THE
NATIONAL MUSEUM
OF CHINA

THE
NATIONAL MUSEUM
OF CHINA

The National Museum of China
London Editions (Hong Kong) Limited

Editor *Lu Zhangshen*
Deputy editors *Huang Zhenchun, Dong Qi*
Editorial team *Guan Shuangxi, Zhu Zhu, Huang Yansheng,*
Wang Guanying, Sheng Weiren, Chen Yu,
Wang Zhan, Yu Lu, Tian Shuai
Jacket image *Dong Qing*
Architect image *Dong Qing*
Photography *Shao Yulan, Dong Qing, Shi Zongping*
Coordinator *Sheng Weiren*
Chinese editor *Yang Ting*
English translation *Susan Whitfield*
English copy editor *Julie Pickard*
English typesetter *Isambard Thomas*
Overall design *Yuan Yinchang, Li Jing*
Planning *Antony White, Cui Jing*

Text and images copyright © 2011
National Museum of China

Edition copyright © 2011 London Editions
(Hong Kong) Limited

Back cover
The Founding Ceremony, 1953 (see no. 321)
Houmuwu square cauldron (*ding*) (see no. 3)

ISBN: 978 1 85759 654 0
First edition 2011
Distributed outside China:
By Scala Publishers
Northburgh House,
10, Northburgh Street
London EC1V 0AT
United Kingdom
Tel: 44 (0) 20 7490 9900

View of National Museum from Jingshan Hill

CONTENTS

ABOUT THE NATIONAL MUSEUM OF CHINA

The National Museum of China was created in February 2003 under the Ministry of Culture by merging the Museum of Chinese History and the Museum of the Chinese Revolution, resulting in a comprehensive national museum for both history and art and for collecting, research, archaeology and cultural exchange.

The forerunner of the Museum of Chinese History was the Preparatory Office of the National Museum founded on 9 July 1912. On 1 October 1949, the same day as the founding of the People's Republic of China, it was renamed the Beijing National History Museum. Its name was changed again in 1959 to the Museum of Chinese History. The origins of the Museum of the Chinese Revolution date back to the establishment of a Preparatory Office of the National Museum of the Revolution in March 1950, which was renamed the Museum of the Chinese Revolution in 1960. In August 1959 two large buildings were completed on the eastern side of Tiananmen Square in Beijing, part of a complex of 10 buildings to commemorate the tenth anniversary of the founding of the People's Republic, and opened on the anniversary, 1 October 1959.

The Museum remains committed to the concept of user-oriented development and growth in order to meet the principle of getting close to the reality of people's lives. The path it follows is commensurate both with China as a world power, with a long and rich history and civilization, and with the development of a modern socialist China meeting the spiritual and cultural needs of the population. The Museum was built to be a leading international institution, to nurture talent, to display great objects, to offer a professional service, and to be a leading academic institution. The Museum, as the leading institution in its area in China, meets the needs of a people, especially the young, to study history, art and culture.

The National Museum Extension Project was carried out from March 2007 to December 2010 resulting in the

construction of an area of 192,000 square metres, creating the world's largest museum and the home for world-class facilities and services. It houses more than 40 galleries, the core display of 'Ancient China' and 'The Road to Revival', as well as 10 different art exhibitions and international loan exhibitions. It therefore not only shows China's own long history and culture and its rejuvenation in the modern period, but also that of world civilization.

PREFACE

The history and art of all aspects of Chinese culture have equal importance, unique among Chinese museums, in the National Museum of China. The museum engages in a complete range of activities, including cultural exchanges. Continually enriched since its beginning in 1912, the collections now present the entire development of Chinese civilization. The National Museum holds a million items in all fields from the prehistoric, through all historical periods, both handed down through generations and discovered through excavation.

The classical Shang and Zhou period bronzes are most important in China and renowned worldwide, reflecting the level in ancient China of ritual and musical systems as well as bronze-making technology. Among the famous Shang bronzes is the so-called Houmuwu (the posthumous name of Fu Hao, consort of the Shang king Wu Ding) *ding*. This is the largest bronze discovered to date, with a high level of modelling, decoration and technique. The recently acquired Zilong cauldron is the largest Shang round cauldron. These are known as the two jewels of Shang bronzes. The Western Zhou Da Yu cauldron bears an inscription of 291 characters, an important historical record. The inscription on the Li *gui* provides important evidence for the transition from the Shang to the Zhou. Another piece, the Ji Zibai *pan* of the state of Guo, is the largest bronze water container from the Shang–Zhou periods, with an inscription of great importance in the research of politics, military affairs and tribal relations in the north in the late Western Zhou. The four-ram square *zun* is an exemplar of Shang art. The collection also contains important pieces such as the Qin Gong *gui*, the *jian* of Fuchai, King of Wu, and the *fou* of Luan Shu. The bronze collection in the museum is comprehensive, including ritual vessels, musical instruments and everyday objects. Several bear inscriptions and are important sources for the study of pre-Qin history.

Other categories of artefacts in the museum's collections also have high artistic and historical value. The ceramics range from pieces with primitive patterns reflecting the life of the time, including the *Jar showing a stork with a fish and a stone axe,* and the *Basin with a fish pattern with a human face*, through to ceramics from the Han to the Tang periods, and tri-coloured glazes of the Tang to porcelains from the kilns of the Song, Yuan, Ming and Qing periods. They include funerary objects, decorative wares and everyday pieces.

Jades form a major part of the collection, diverse and rich in form and type, ranging from a Hongshan Culture dragon from the tomb of Fu Hao, to the Western Han gold sewn jade suit and a Sui gold-rimmed jade cup.

In painting and calligraphy, the paintings have particular historical interest. *Offering Tribute* and T*he Four Generals of Zhongxing* from the Song, the Ming *Thriving Southern Capital* and the *Qing Southern Inspection Tour of Qianlong* are of an unsurpassed artistic quality as National Treasures, and illustrate contemporary society.

Gold and silverware show both ancient Chinese techniques and multiculturalism. The numismatic collection has a large outstanding exhibition room thanks to donations from great collectors of the 1950s and 1960s, such as Luo Bozhao and Shen Zicha. Historical seals are source material for ancient politics. Pictorial bricks show everyday life in ancient China.

These artefacts show the state of Chinese society at various times, the technology and aesthetics, and reveal Chinese history from economic, political and cultural aspects. The Museum's collections contain treasures from the entire country. They are concrete examples of China's economic development, society, science, technology, art and the history of its many peoples. This catalogue presents the essence of the collections to its readers and hopes that it will give them both enjoyment and inspiration.

Lu Zhangshen   Director of the National Museum of China

HISTORICAL TIMES

BRONZES

China has a long and lustrous history of bronze art, lasting 4000 years from the Xia period to today. The National Museum collection ranges from the pre-Qin period to the Ming and Qing, and contains treasures from all parts of the country. Not only is it a very large collection, it also includes all types of bronzes, including vessels, weapons, musical instruments, implements, agricultural tools, horse and chariot fittings and all sorts of everyday objects. As a manifestation of the politics, economics, culture and life of their time this is an important repository for the study of history, art and technology, and a precious cultural heritage for the development of human civilization.

Bronze technology reached its maturity during the Shang. New forms developed, among them the most important food vessels were the *ding, yan and gui*, and the most common wine vessels the *jue* and *gu*. All had a ritual function. The decoration developed from crude simple patterns to finer and more elaborate designs, the animal face becoming in this time the most important decoration, with supplementary patterns such as the cloud and thunder pattern and geometrical designs. The Museum's collection includes bronzes from the tomb of Fu Hao at Anyang, Henan – the double *fang yi*, the three-bowl steamer, the owl-shaped *zun*, the Houmuwu *ding* and the square *jia* – with their unusual shapes and exquisite decoration, representing the very best of bronze art from the Shang period. It also holds the four-ram *zun* from Ningxiang, Hunan and the dragon and tiger *zun* from Funan, Anhui, which combine high relief with dense background engraving, giving prominence to the main design and a sense of layers. Among those pieces made using multiple casting techniques, large-scale bronzes are common, the National Museum having the one-metre high square *ding* with nipple pattern excavated at Zhengzhou, Henan, as well as the Houmuwu square *ding*, weighing 833 kg.

In the Western Zhou period, bronze art developed in new directions. Ritual vessels displayed new characteristics, the use of ritual sets centred on the *ding* gradually becoming established, but combined more often with water vessels such as the *pan* and the *he* rather than wine vessels. New forms appeared, including the *xu* and *fu*, both food vessels, and the *yi*, a water vessel. At the same time, there was a tendency for vessels to become squatter with drooping bellies. Representative of design at this time are the crested phoenix bird and the dragon. It also became more common for long inscriptions to be cast on the bronze, with a rich content extremely valuable for researching Western Zhou politics, economics and society.

In the Spring and Autumn period the power of the Zhou kings declined and individual kingdoms/states became more powerful; gradually each developed their own artistic forms and styles. Bronzes went through great changes, with new forms of the *dui* among food vessels and the *jian* and others among water vessels. Fine tight hornless dragon patterns became dominant. The Museum's collection includes examples from all the states.

During the Warring States period bronze technology and art reached new heights with the use of the lost-wax method and stamped patterning. At this time vessels were made in singular shapes with intricate designs and meticulous workmanship. The most popular patterns were depictions of humans, the hornless dragon and flowers. Techniques such as gold plating, inlaid gold and silver and painting with lacquer were used, producing innovative visual effects. Vessels from this period in the Museum's collections include the Heir to the Lord of Linghu *hu*, Chu Gao *fou*, Ejun Qi tally, the combined *fou* and *jian* from Marquis Yi's tomb.

From the Qin and Han periods, bronze was mainly used for everyday objects, and in the Han the techniques of inlaid gold and silver and coloured patterns predominated. The vessel with the sacrifice scene and the *Seven-ox vessel for storing cowries* reflect the customs of the Western Han Dian peoples (from present-day Yunnan). (Su Qiang)

2

Square cauldron (*ding*) with nipple pattern

Early Shang (1600–1300 BC)

Height 100 cm, Mouth 62.5 x 61 cm

Excavated in 1974 at Zhangzhainanlu, Zhengzhou, Henan Province

3

Houmuwu square cauldron (*ding*)

Late Shang (1300–1046 BC)

Height 133 cm, Mouth 112 x 79.2 cm

Said to have been excavated in 1939 at Wuguancun, Anyang, Henan Province

1

Mirror with double wheel and star design

Neolithic, Qijia Culture (2500–1500 BC)

Diameter 14.6 cm, Thickness 0.15 cm

Said to have been excavated in Gansu Province

This piece, which was called Simuwu, is a rectangular vessel with a protruding rim and thick square lip. It has two large upright arched handles, one of which has been replaced. The cauldron has straight sides, a deep belly and a flat base, and four hollow cylindrical feet. There are shallow flanges on the face and corners of the body. The top and bottom of the body bears an animal face design with a coiled tail; there are animal faces and one-legged dragon designs on the four edges with a base design of clouds and thunder. The design on the outer part of the handles shows two facing tigers with a human head in their mouths, with fish on the edges. The upper part of the feet bear an animal face, with a three-cord design below.

Three characters are inscribed on the inside of the body: 'Hou mu wu', written in a vigorous and robust script, with full shape and strokes which taper into points at their ends but are full in the middle. 'Mu' was the posthumous name of Fu Hao, consort of the Shang king Wu Ding. Her tomb is the best preserved of the Shang royal tombs, containing over 400 bronzes. The vessel was made on order of Fu Hao's son, also a Shang king, to carry out rituals for his mother (mu) – her surname was Wu. An alternative name is the Houmuwu *ding*. It is substantial and powerful yet remains elegant with a beautiful design, showing a superb level of casting, and is the largest Shang ritual bronze vessel found to date. (Su Qiang)

4

Fu Hao steamer (*yan*) with three bowls (*zeng*)

Late Shang (1300–1046 BC)

Overall Height 68 cm, Length 103.7 cm, Width 27 cm, Height of top section 26.2 cm,
Mouth 33 cm, Base Diameter 15 cm

Excavated in 1976 from the tomb of Fu Hao, Anyang, Henan Province

Yan is a vessel for steaming food and is in two parts, the upper part, or *zeng*, used for placing the food for steaming, and the lower part for holding the boiling water. There are perforations in between to allow the steam to rise. This vessel comprises three round bowls on a rectangular lower part. The bowls are very slightly curved with wide mouths and two semi-circular handles decorated with ox faces. There is a depression on the inside base with three fan-shaped holes. There is a band below the rims, with a design of facing one-legged dragons separated by a flange on a ground of thunder patterns with whirlpool patterns above and below the bodies of the dragons.

The lower part has three raised round openings, a hollow body, flat base and stands on six feet. There is a design of triangles and clouds on the circumference wall of the raised openings. Three groups of coiled dragons wind around the face with ox faces on the four corners. The four sides show one-legged dragons in between raised whirlpool designs, with a big triangular design below and a ground of cloud and thunder design. The two characters 'Fu Hao' are inscribed on the inside wall of the middle raised round opening of the lower section, on the inside of its body and on the outer wall below the two ear handles. This is a very distinctive piece, unique among Shang-period bronzes. Fu Hao was the consort of the Shang king Wu Ding, and a prominent member of the ruling and military Shang dynasty. (Su Qiang)

5

Fu Hao square wine vessel (*jia*)

Late Shang (1300–1046 BC)

Height 68.8 cm, Mouth 25.1 x 24 cm

Excavated in 1976 from the tomb of Fu Hao, Anyang, Henan Province

6

Fu Hao owl-shaped vessel (*zun*)

Late Shang (1300–1046 BC)

Height 46.3 cm, Mouth 16.1 cm

Excavated in 1976 from the tomb of Fu Hao, Anyang, Henan Province

Side view

7

Fu Hao paired vessel (*fang yi*)

Late Shang (1300–1046 BC)
Height 60 cm, Mouth 88.2 cm x 17.5 cm
*Excavated in 1976 from the tomb of Fu Hao,
Anyang, Henan Province*

The *y*i is a wine vessel fashionable from the late Shang to the early Western Zhou, and usually has a rectangular shape, with a roof-shaped lid, a square or curved belly, and a ring foot. This square *y*i is a unique piece, resembling a combination of two *fang yi*, hence its name, 'paired *fang yi*'. The mouth, belly, feet and lid are all rectangular. It has a square lip, a slightly concave shoulder, and convex belly with straight ends on which there are ring ear handles. The base is flat and the rectangular-shaped high ring foot flares out very slightly. There is a raised opening on all four sides of the foot. It has flanges on the central part of the four sides of the body, on the four corners and on the foot, and on the long side of the body are seven protruding beam-like hemispherical sections. Below the mouth on both sides is a protruding head of a sacrificial animal with a small bird design on either side. The central part of the belly on the long sides is decorated with a large animal face design, with the flange as its nose, protruding round eyes, an open mouth, small ears and curly horns. On each side of its mouth is a dragon and

bird design, the ends of which further divide and turn into one-legged dragons. Above the handles on the short ends are protruding elephant heads with owl designs on either side and a large animal face design below.

The lid resembles a ridged roof with pillar-shaped knobs on top. There are flanges on the ridge, the four corners and the middle of all four sides. On the long side are seven protrusions that slot over the seven beam sections on the body. The lip at each short end of the lid also fits over the body. There are two inverted one-legged dragons on both short ends of the lid. The roof pillars are decorated with triangles and zigzags. On the middle of each long side of the ring foot is a protruding design of a pair of back-to-back coiled snakes and animal face designs on the edges of the long and short sides, with the flange as a nose, a T-shaped horn, open mouth and coiled tail. Under the base is a two-character inscription reading 'Fu Hao'.

This large-scale wine vessel is a fine example of Yinxu-period Shang bronze ware. (Su Qiang)

9

Animal face ax

Late Shang (1300–1046 BC)
Length 31.7 cm, Width 35.8 cm

*Excavated in 1965 from Subutun,
Yidu (present-day Qingzhou),
Shandong Province*

8

Simuxin *gong*

Late Shang (1300–1046 BC)
Height 36 cm, Length 46.5 cm, Width 12.5 cm
*Excavated in 1976 from the tomb of Fu Hao,
Anyang, Henan Province*

11
Chime bell with elephant design
Late Shang (1300–1046 BC)
Height 69.5 cm, Width 56.5 cm

10
Zuoceban turtle
Late Shang (1300–1046 BC)
Height 10 cm, Length 21.4 cm, Width 16 cm

12

Dragon and tiger vessel (*zun*)

Late Shang (1300–1046 BC)

Height 50.5 cm,
Diameter at mouth 44.7 cm,
Diameter at foot 24 cm

*Excavated in 1957 from Yueyahe,
Funan, Anhui Province*

This is a tall and large *zun*, with a trumpet-shaped mouth, girded neck, broad sloping shoulder, belly which narrows at the bottom, and a high ring foot. The neck is decorated with three narrow bands, the shoulder with three protruding wriggling dragons with upright conical horns, open mouths, extended bodies and coiled tail. Behind their tails is another small dragon design. The belly has a design of a tiger, with raised head in high relief and bodies in shallower relief, extending on both sides of the head. Below the tiger's head is a squatting man with arms raised above his shoulders, his head inside the jaw of the tiger. Below both designs is an animal face design with the corner flange of the vessel forming its nose, T-shaped horns and a scrolled tail. The ring foot has three cross-shaped piercings and, on the lower part, animal face designs. The mixture of the techniques of engraving, high relief and three-dimensional relief on the shoulder and belly combined with the delicate and beautiful designs make this a masterpiece of Shang bronze work. In ancient times, non-Chinese peoples lived in Huaiyi Region, where this piece was excavated, and it shows the influence of Shang bronzes combined with local features.
(Su Qiang)

13

Square vessel (*fang zun*) with four rams

Late Shang (1300–1046 BC)
Height 58.3 cm, Mouth 52.4 cm
Excavated in 1938 from Yueshanpu, Ningxiang, Hunan Province

This square *zun* has a generous mouth with a flared flat lip, a long neck, projecting shoulder, shallow belly and high ring foot. There are flanges on the four corners and in the middle of all four sides. The neck has a design of triangular one-legged dragons and the flanges become the noses of the animal face designs below, with curly horns, round protruding eyes and a scrolled tail. On the shoulder are high-relief designs of dragons with their three-dimensional heads on the centre and their bodies wriggling along the sides. On the four corners of the shoulder are four protruding rams' heads with curly horns, the belly of the vessel forming their chests and their

legs extending down the ring foot. Their heads have engraved thunder patterns while there are scales on their chests and backs. Both sides are decorated with an elegant design of a bird with a high crest. The ring foot also carries a design of one-legged dragons. This vessel combines the techniques of engraving, high relief and three-dimensional relief in a dignified and refined form with intricately worked designs. It is a perfect fusion of moulding and artistic design representing the very best of bronze-making by the traditional clay mould technique. (Su Qiang)

14

Zilong cauldron (*ding*)

Late Shang (1300–1046 BC)

Height 103 cm, Mouth 80 cm, Weight 230 kg

Said to have been excavated in the 1920s from Huixian, Henan Province

This *ding* has a thick and heavy body, with upright ear handles, a protruding square lip, deep belly, which is pinched in below, a curved base and hoof-shaped feet. The main body has a design of six paired animal faces, one with a body and one without, with alternating cloud and thunder designs. The animal faces have a ridged nose and the legs bear a design of horned rams' heads. This is an imposing piece, both elegant yet powerful, with well-ordered designs, and is the largest Shang-period round *ding* discovered to date. It reflects the high level of late Shang bronze technology and art. The characters cast into the inside read 'Zilong', the character for 'long' being a simplified form of the character for 'gong'. According to historical sources, 'gong' is an ancient name for Hui County in Henan Province, the place where this *ding* was excavated. The Zilong were a powerful clan in this area at the end of the Shang, with the means to make such a large *ding*. (Tian Shuai)

15

Mask with protruding eyes

Late Shang (1300–1046 BC)
Height 85.4 cm, Width 78 cm
*Excavated in 1986 at Sanxingdui,
Guanghan, Sichuan Province*

This is a mask used in sacrificial offerings. Rectangular in form, it has dagger-shaped thick eyebrows, cylindrical protruding eyes, a curved nose, large upturned mouth with the tongue showing, and spear-shaped ears drawn out on either side.

There is a high ornament over the nose and forehead, with a pointed spiral at the top and bottom and knife-shaped wing in the middle. This piece embodies the spirit of the peoples of ancient Shu (present-day Sichuan Province), and is probably an image of the legendary creator of sericulture, Cancong. (Su Qiang)

16

Li vessel (*gui*)

Early Western Zhou (c.11th–10th centuries BC)
Height 28 cm, Mouth 22 cm
Excavated in 1976 in Lintong, Shanxi Province

The *gui* is for holding grains such as millet and rice and for warming food. An important ritual vessel, it was often used together with a cauldron or *ding*. This one has a wide mouth, nipped-in neck and deep belly extending down to a ring foot sitting on a square base. It has two semi-circular animal head handles, with horns extending above the rim and rectangular earrings hanging below. The body and base have a thunder pattern design decorated with animal faces with scrolled horns, circular protruding eyes and open mouths; at the top centre of each face is the face of a sacrificial animal. On the base there is a one-legged dragon on each side of the animal face design and a cicada design on the corner. The ring foot has pairs of facing one-legged dragons separated by flanges.

On the inside of the base is a four-line, 32-character inscription of great historical importance recording the campaigns of King Wu against the Shang, from the early triumphs when the Zhou seized power. It is the earliest Western Zhou bronze found to date. (Su Qiang)

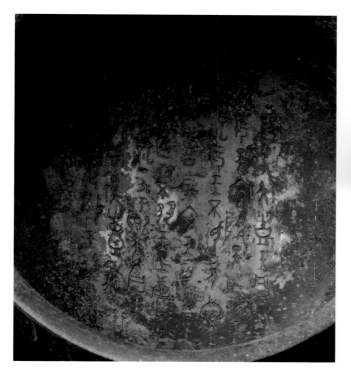

17

Tianwang vessel (*gui*)

Early Western Zhou (c.11th–10th centuries BC)

Height 24.2 cm, Mouth 21 cm

*Said to have been excavated during the
Daoguang period (1821–1850) in Qishan,
Shaanxi Province*

18

Marquis of Yi Ze vessel (*gui*)

Early Western Zhou (c.11th–10th centuries BC)

Height 15.7 cm, Mouth 22.5 cm

*Excavated in 1954 Yandunshan, Dantu,
Jiangsu Province*

19

Marquis of Yan vessel (*yu*)

Early Western Zhou (c.11th–10th centuries BC)
Height 24.5 cm, Mouth 33.8 cm,
Diameter at base 23.3 cm
*Excavated in 1955 in Ling Yuan City,
Liaoning Province*

This vessel has a round body, slightly flared mouth with a wide lip, and a deep belly with ear handles on either side linked to the vessel at their top by a small rod. The base is flat and there is a high ring foot. The base design is of thunder patterns decorated with one-legged dragons. The dragons' heads are adorned with a splendid crest which hangs down. Inside the vessel is an inscription of five characters recording that this vessel was made for the Marquis of Yan.

The *yu* vessel to hold either water or cooked rice appeared at the end of the Shang period and became popular in the Western Zhou. Based on the inscription, this vessel was used in the state of Yan. Yan was an important feudal state in the north in the early Zhou period, and the fact that this piece was discovered in Liaoning Province demonstrates that the power of the Yan already extended to the Liao River by this time. (Su Qiang)

20

Da Yu cauldron (Da Yu *ding*)

Early Western Zhou (c.11th–10th centuries BC)
Height 101.9 cm, Diameter at mouth 77.8 cm
Said to have been excavated in the Daoguang reign period (1821–50) in Meixian, Shaanxi Province, and gifted by Pan Dayu in 1951

This cauldron has a circular body, a restrained mouth, wide flat lip with protuding rim and a pair of upright ear handles. Below is a nipped-in neck, drooping belly and three cylindrical legs. There are six curved horn animal face designs below the rim and on the legs, the corner flange of the leg acting as the nose, and with a cloud and thunder design as the base. Inside is an inscription of 291 characters in 19 lines.

Cast bronze cauldrons were often in pairs. Originally there was a small Yu cauldron (Xiao Yu *ding*) as well as this large one, but it is no longer extant and only a rubbing of its inscription survives. The Da Yu *ding* is a famous treasure of the early Western Zhou, with its imposing and dignified modelling, inscription in a vigorous hand, and important historical value. (Su Qiang)

21

Duck-shaped wine vessel (*zun*)

Early Western Zhou (c.11th–10th centuries BC)

Height 44.6 cm, Length 41.9 cm,
Diameter at mouth 12.7 cm

*Excavated in 1955 from Lingyuan City,
Liaoning Province*

23

Zi Cauldron (*gui*)

Early Western Zhou (c.11th–10th centuries BC)

Height 17 cm, Diameter at mouth 18.5 cm

22

Shao wine vessel (*you*)

Early Western Zhou (c.11th–10th centuries BC)

Height 9.5 cm, Diameter 9.6 cm, Diameter at foot, 9.7 cm

24

Li horse-shaped wine vessel (*zun*)

Mid Western Zhou (c.10th–9th centuries BC)
Height 32 cm, Length 33 cm
*Excavated in 1955 from Meixian,
Shaanxi Province*

This vessel is in the form of a standing colt with raised head,
its ears pricked and a cropped mane and tail. It is hollow and
there is a rectangular hole in its back with a small lid bearing
an animal knob. The horse's side is decorated with a whirlpool
design. There is a nine-line inscription of 94 characters on
the front of its neck that records horse-herding ceremonies.
The modelling is realistic, demonstrating the excellent casting
techniques in China during the Western Zhou. (Su Qiang)

25

Li wine vessel (square *yi*)

Mid Western Zhou (c.10th–9th centuries BC)
Height 22.8 cm, Mouth 14.3 cm x 10.9 cm
Excavated in 1955 from Mexian, Shaanxi Province

26

Set of Zhangxin chime bells

Mid Western Zhou
(c.10th–9th centuries BC)

Heights 48.5, 44 and 38 cm,
Widths 27.5, 25 and 21 cm
Excavated in 1954 in Puducun, Chang'an, Shaanxi Province

27

Gebo food vessel (*gui*)

Mid Western Zhou (c.10th–9th centuries BC)
Height 31 cm, Diameter at mouth 21.4 cm,
Width of base 18.9 cm

28

Shiyou food vessel (*gui*)

Late Western Zhou (c.9th century–771 BC)
Height 22.5 cm, Diameter at mouth 19.1 cm,
Diameter at foot 20 cm

29

Yu cauldron (*ding*)

Late Western Zhou (c.9th century to 771 BC)
Height 54.6 cm, Diameter at mouth 46.7 cm

*Excavated in 1942 at Renjiacun, Fufeng,
Shaanxi Province*

30

Song flask (*hu*)

Late Western Zhou (c.9th century–771 BC)
(vessel from the time of King Xuan of the
Zhou and so dating from the later part of
this period)

Height 51 cm

This oblate wine vessel has an open
mouth with an inward-turned lip and
animal head handles with rings on either
side of the neck. The oblate belly is low
and supported on a ring foot. The neck
has a wave design while the body bears
a design of dragons sharing one head
between two bodies. The foot shows
hanging scales. There is an inscription of
152 characters on the inside of the neck,
recording in detail the complete lineage
of rulers and is therefore of immense
importance for the study of Western
Zhou ruling system. (Su Qiang)

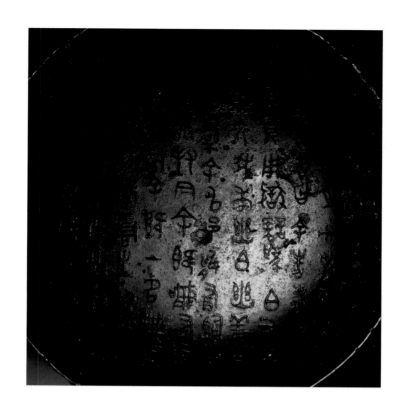

31

Diaosheng food vessel (*gui*)

Late Western Zhou (c.9th century–771 BC)

Height 22.2 cm, Diameter at mouth 21.9 cm

Donated in 1959 by Zhang Shaoming

32

Guo Ji Zibai water vessel (*pan*)

Late Western Zhou (c.9th century–771 BC)

Height 39.5 cm, Length 137.2 cm, Width 86.5 cm

Excavated in the Daoguang reign period (1821–50) at Baoji, Shaanxi Province, and donated by Liu Suceng in 1950

The *pan* is a water vessel in common use from the late Western Zhou period, which from this time is found in a set with a water jug. This piece is famous as the largest *pan* extant from the pre-Qin period. Rectangular shaped with rounded corners, it has a square lip, deep belly with a flat bottom and four rectangular feet. Each side has a pair of ring handles held by animal heads, the animals having short horns, thick eyebrows and round eyes. The ring handles are moulded like ropes. There is a curved pattern below the rim and a wave band on the body below. On the bottom is an inscription of 110 characters in eight lines written in rhyming four-character phrases. After this vessel was originally unearthed it was used as a feeding tray for horses, but was later reburied for protection and then dug up by Liu Sucheng and presented to the government. Not only is this piece very interesting for its historical content, but it is also a literary masterpiece. (Su Qiang)

33

Zeng Zhong You Fu square flask (*hu*)

Early Spring and Autumn (770–671 BC)

Height 65.5 cm, Mouth 22.8 x 16.5 cm, Foot 30.5 x 23.5 cm

Excavated in 1966 from Sujialong, Jingshanxian, Hubei Province

34

Mirror with design of birds and beasts

Western Zhou–Spring and Autumn (8th century BC)

Diameter 6.7 cm, Thickness 0.35 cm

Excavated in 1957 from a Guo tomb, Shangcunling, Sanmenxia, Henan Province

35

Vessel (*zun*) in the form
of a sacrificial animal

Early Spring and Autumn (770–671 BC)
Height 29 cm, Length 31.5 cm
*Excavated in 1956 from Shangcunling,
Sanmenxia, Henan Province*

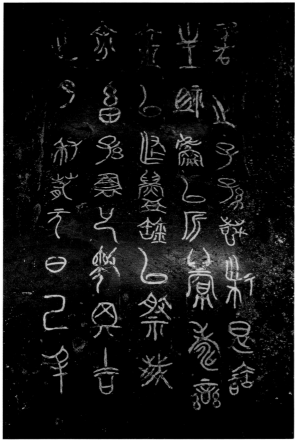

36

Luan Shu vessel (*fou*)

Mid Spring and Autumn (670–571 BC)
Height 40.8 cm, Diameter at mouth 16.5 cm

Fou vessels are divided into *zunfou* and *yufou*, wine vessels and water vessels. This is one of the former, a wine vessel, and is in two parts, the body and the lid. The convex lid bears four ring knobs. The vessel has a straight neck, wide spreading shoulders, a convex belly and flat base. There are four loop handles on the body. The lid knobs and handles have a design of angular clouds. The body is unadorned.

There is an inscription of 40 characters in five lines running from the neck on to the shoulder. It records that this vessel was made for Luan Shu's descendants to offer sacrifices to their forbears. The inscription is inlaid with gold, as is typically seen on weapons but usually with fewer characters than here, making this a very rare piece. The gold sparkles, the characters are elegant, neatly written, reflecting the level of bronze making in the Jin state during the Spring and Autumn period and making this an important piece for studying the warfare of the time. (Su Qiang)

37

Wangzi yingci tray (*lu*)

Mid Spring and Autumn (670–571 BC)
Height 12.2 cm, Length 45.4 cm, Width 35.6 cm
*Said to have been excavated in 1923 from Lijialou,
Xindeng, Henan Province*

38

Duke of Qin vessel (*gui*)

Mid Spring and Autumn (670–571 BC)
Height 19.8 cm, Diameter at mouth 18 cm
Said to have been excavated in 1919 from Tianshui, Gansu Province

Made for Jing Gong which was the king of Qin state during the Spring and Autumn period to use in sacrificial rituals to his ancestors. The body has a band design, and the rest of the body and lid are both covered with a design of coiled snakes. It has a flared ring foot and ring handles in the form of animal heads. Inside the vessel and lid is an inscription of 123 characters. The specific characteristics of this vessel are apparent in the inscription, which has been made by stamping so that the rectangular frame of the stamp can be seen around each character. This technique is unique to this piece among all extant Shang and Zhou bronzes. The inscription records the 12 generations of the rulers of the Qin state, and the great achievements of the Duke of Jing's predecessors in enriching the people and their military campaigns; it appeals to the ancestors for good fortune and to protect and bring peace to the Qin state and the gods of earth and grain for all time. (Tian Shuai)

39

Wang Ziwu cauldron (*ding*)

Late Spring and Autumn (570–476 BC)

Height 67 cm, Diameter at mouth 66 cm,
Diameter at belly 68 cm

*Excavated in 1978 from Xiasi,
Zhechuanxian, Henan Province*

40

Duke Hua of Zhu bell

Late Spring and Autumn (570–476 BC)
Length 36.4 cm, Width 18.1 cm
Excavated from Zouxian, Shandong Province

41

Huanzi Mengjiang flask (*hu*)

Late Spring and Autumn (570–476 BC)

Height 32.2, Diameter at mouth 13.4 cm,
Diameter at foot 18.7 cm

42

Cai Hou Shen square vase (*fang hu*)

Late Spring and Autumn (570–476 BC)

Height 79.8 cm, Mouth 18.5 x 18.3 cm

*Excavated in 1955 from Marquis Cai's tomb, Shouxian,
Anhui Province*

43

King Guang of Wu's vessel (*jian*)

Late Spring and Autumn (570–476 BC)

Height 35.5 cm, Diameter at mouth 57.7 cm,
Diameter at base 32 cm

*Excavated in 1955 from Marquis Cai's tomb,
Shouxian, Anhui Province*

44

King Fuchai of Wu vessel (*jian*)

Late Spring and Autumn (570–476 BC)
Height 45.5 cm, Diameter at mouth 76.6 cm,
Diameter at base 47.2 cm
*Said to have been excavated from Liulige,
Huixian, Henan Province*

This is a water vessel, but can be used for
both holding water (and seeing one's face
reflected in the water) or for holding iced
food. This form of huge *jian* was used either
in ritual or for display. It has a spacious
mouth, square protruding lip, a nipped-in
neck, deep convex belly and a flat base.
The two handles on either side of the
neck are rings held in the mouth of animal
heads with two disks hanging from them.
In between are two bow-shaped crouching
tigers in relief that are climbing up the
vessel looking over the rim. The body has a
complex and dense design of coiled snakes
with triangles below enclosing more coiled
snakes. Inside the belly is an inscription of
13 characters in two lines that records that
this vessel was made for King Fuchai of Wu.
(Su Qiang)

46

Vessel (*zun*) with a decoration of a snake devouring a frog

Late Spring and Autumn (570–476 BC)

Height 16.2 cm, Diameter at mouth 17 cm, Diameter at foot 12.2 cm

Excavated in 1971 at Gongcheng, Guangxi Zhuang Automonous Region

45

Bird-shaped cauldron (*ding*)

Late Spring and Autumn (570–476 BC)

Height 16 cm, Length 22.9 cm

Excavated in 1952 at Jiagezhuang, Tangshan, Hebei Province

47

Snake and frog patterned hoop-handled vessel (*you*)

Late Spring and Autumn (570–476 BC)

Height 49 cm, Length at mouth 27.2 cm, Width at mouth 19.5 cm

Excavated in 1986 at Xiangtan, Hunan Province

48

**Double animal head bowl (*pan*)
with three wheels**

Late Spring and Autumn (570–476 BC)

Height 15.8 cm, Diameter 26 cm,
Diameter at base 14.5 cm

*Excavated in 1957 from Yancheng, Wujinxian,
Jiangsu Province*

This shallow bowl has a wide mouth with a protruding rim, a curved body and a circular base. Attached to the base is a handle in the form of two animals with protruding mouths and a pointed horn on their heads that are facing the water in the bowl. Between them is a wheel and there are two other wheels attached to the base. The wheels have six spokes and are functional. There is a braided design on the outside of the body that is similar to the stamped design found on pottery. The necks of the animals are decorated with a scale design with a pair of wings at their waist. This piece was part of a set of sacrificial animal heads. It shows ingenious modelling yet is practical. Its regional origins are obvious, being a representative bronze of the Wu state during the Spring and Autumn period. (Su Qiang)

49

Wine vessel (*fou*) and ice basin (*jian*)

Early Warring States (475–376 BC)
Height 63.2 cm, Diameter at mouth 63 cm
*Excavated in 1978 from the tomb of Marquis Yi of Zeng
state at Leigudun, Suixian, Hubei Province*

This is a combination of a square water vessel (*jian*) with a covered square wine vessel (*zunfou*) inside. The water vessel has a vertical mouth with a squared rim, a deep belly, a rimmed foot and four animal-shaped feet. Symmetrically placed on the belly and the four corners are eight bow-shaped handles formed of dragons with curly tails and a square-shaped decoration on the crowns of their heads. It has an openwork engraved lid with a square hole in the centre and ring handles on the four sides. A lidded square wine vessel sits inside, also with a vertical mouth, sloping shoulder, deep belly and round feet. On the four corners of its square lid are four ring knobs and there are ring handles on each of the four sides and feet.

L-shaped hooks protrude from the base of the outer basin and fit into holes on the feet of the wine vessel holding it in place and preventing movement. Ice is placed in the space between the two vessels both to cool and to preserve the wine.

The decoration of the set is complex with coiled dragons and shapes morphing into dragons, linked clouds and plantain leaf designs reflecting a diversity of techniques including engraving, bold relief and three-dimensional decoration. There is a seven-character inscription, 'Forever used by Marquis Yi of Zeng'. When excavated it was found with a long-handled ladle with two hoops on the end of handle and completely decorated with cloud designs. (Su Qiang)

50

Heir to the Lord of Linghu flask (*hu*)

Early Warring States (5th–4th centuries BC)

Height 46.5 cm, Diameter at mouth 14.8 cm,

Diameter at base 16.8 cm

*Said to have been excavated in 1927 from Jincun,
Luoyang, Henan Province*

51

Man-shaped lamp stand with spoon

Mid Warring States (375–276 BC)
Height 23.9 cm, Diameter of bowl 11.5 cm,
Length of spoon 22.7 cm

*Excavated in 1957 in Gebukoucun, Zhucheng,
Shandong Province*

The powerful figure wearing a short tunic and with head raised is standing on a disk in the form of a coiled dragon. His right arm is held horizontally, his left slightly lowered and in both hands he is holding a lamp support in the form of bent bamboo with leaves, slotted into the upper part of which are oil lamps in the form of circular trays. This piece was found together with a long-handled oval spoon with a flat end and animal designs used to add oil. It is an ingenious design in a new and original style, combining pragmatism and art and most probably was used in the court of the Qi state during the Warring States period. (Su Qiang)

52

Ejun Qi tallies (*jie*)

Mid Warring States (375–276 BC)

Lengths 31 and 29.6 cm, Width of each 7.3 cm, Thickness of each 0.7 cm

Excavated in 1957 from Shouxian, Anhui Province

53

Openwork animal-patterned brazier (*xun*)

Late Warring States (275–221 BC)

Height 14 cm, Diameter at mouth 11.8 cm

Excavated in 1957 at Changtaiguan, Xinyang, Henan Province

54

Jing Li Set of bells (13 pieces)

Late Warring States (275–221 BC)

Height 13–30.5 cm, Width 6.4–17 cm

Excavated in 1957 from Chu tomb at Changtaiguan, Xinyang, Henan Province

55

Chu Gao wine vessel (*fou*)

Late Warring States (275–221 BC)

Height 27 cm, Diameter at mouth 24.5 cm,
Diameter at base 24.1 cm

*Excavated in 1954 from Gengdaocun,
Tai'an, Shandong Province*

56

**King of Chu Xiong Han
cauldron (*ding*)**

Warring States (475–221 BC)

Height 53.5 cm, Diameter at mouth 55.4 cm

*Excavated in 1933 from Zhujiaji, Shouxian,
Anhui Province*

57

Mirror decorated with six mountain characters

Late Warring States (275–221 BC)
Diameter 23.2 cm, Thickness 0.6 cm

58

Mirror decorated with warriors and leopards

Late Warring States to Qin (275–206 BC)

Diameter 10.4 cm, Thickness 0.2 cm

Excavated in 1975 from tomb No. 9, Shuihu, Yunmeng, Hubei Province

The mirror has a knob of three strings inside a double square and a background double thunder pattern. It depicts two warriors, barefoot and with naked torsos, wearing helmets, with a sword in their right hand and a shield in their left, depicted in a vivid manner confronting two leopards. This is a portrayal of the martial spirit of the Qin peoples at the time. (Sheng Weiren)

59

**Gold-inlaid bird character
vessel (*hu*)**

Western Han (206 BC – AD 8)

Height 44.2 cm,
Diameter at mouth 15.1 cm,
Diameter at belly 28.5 cm

*Excavated in 1968 from the tomb of
Liusheng, Prince Jing, at Zhongshan,
Mancheng, Hebei*

60

**Vessel (*zun*) with gold-plated
bird and beast design**

Western Han (206 BC – AD 8)

Height 20 cm, Diameter 19.7 cm

This lamp is in the form of a goose with its head turned back and holding a fish in its mouth, made of four dismantable sections, namely the goose head and long neck, the body, the lamp tray and the lamp shade. The goose neck part slots into its body and the body of the fish; the goose neck and body are hollow; the bottom of the fish body joins the arch-shaped cover, the upper part of which is inserted into the opening below the fish's belly; and the lower section of this is inserted into the lamp shade, which opens by sliding sideways so adjusting the brightness and angle of the light. The cover is slightly curved, one side attached to the lamp shaft allowing the tray to be turned. The ring foot of the lamp slots into a hold on the back of the goose's body. The smoke and dust passes through the fish and the goose's neck into the hollow body and finally dissolves in water.

Lamps made in the Han period are diverse in form, for example, wild goose foot, a recumbent sheep, the mythical Vermillion Bird and an ox. This lamp uses a traditional form of a bird with a fish in its mouth. The goose has a crest, round eyes, a long neck, plump body, short tail and webbed feet. The crest is painted red, the goose and fish body are in green, with the wings and the scales outlined in ink. With its lively form, ingenious design and gorgeous decoration it perfectly combines function and form. (Su Qiang)

61

Painted goose and fish lamp

Western Han (206 BC – AD 8)
Height 53 cm, Length 34.5 cm
Excavated in 1985 from Pingshou, Shanxi Province

62

Gold and silver inlay cloud-patterned rhinoceros vessel (*zun*)

Western Han (206 BC – AD 8)
Height 34.4 cm, Length 58.1 cm
Excavated in 1963 from Doumacun, Xingping, Shaanxi Province

This vessel is in the form of a powerful standing rhinoceros with a raised head with pricked ears and sharp tusks. Its eyes are bright black glass beads, giving it a graceful expression. The lid on its back is hinged at the front allowing it to be opened. Cloud decorations cover the entire body with spirals in between, all inlaid with gold and silver, suggesting the fine hairs of the rhinoceros. This is a realistic piece with flowing and lively decoration, and deserves to be considered a masterpiece of Western Han gold and silver inlay. (Su Qiang)

63

Storage vessel for cowries with scene of a sacrifice

Western Han (206 BC – AD 8)

Height 53 cm, Diameter at lid 32 cm, Diameter at base 29.7 cm

Excavated in 1957 from Shizhaishan, Jining, Yunnan Province

The vessel is in the form of a waisted drum with a flat base and three animal-claw feet. The two handles are formed from tigers. A flat lid supports a scene of sacrificial ceremony and swearing of allegiances. On one side is a raised covered platform supported by two massive pillars. This platform has a roof made of poles that cross at the ridge. Underneath this platform is a woman, seated higher than the others, possibly the main sacrificer. There are 16 drums in two rows. The figures, animals, apparatus and instruments are all tightly packed and entangled on the platform. Among them are butchers, animal handlers, musicians, banqueters, those offering tribute and those making human sacrifices. This large and technically complicated piece was made by the lost-wax method, and has up to 127 figures. It is an important piece for studying the society of the Dian peoples (in present-day Yunnan) in the Han period. (Su Qiang)

64

Seven-ox vessel for storing cowries

Western Han (206 BC – AD 8)

Height 44 cm, Diameter at mouth 16.7 cm,
Diameter at base 21.6 cm

*Excavated in 1957 from Shizhaishan,
Jining, Yunnan Province*

65

Five-ox pillow

Western Han (206 BC – AD 8)

Height 15.5 cm, Length 50.3 cm,
Width 10.6 cm

*Excavated in 1972 from Lijiashan,
Jiangchuan, Yunnan Province*

In its form this piece resembles a saddle, with raised rounded
ends on each of which stands a cast bronze ox, well fed,
powerful in posture and with upright horns. The top of the
pillow is smooth and flat. There are three oxen depicted on one
side with their heads in relief and, in the gaps between them,
a design of snakes and tigers, each in a different pose. The
people of the Dian Culture (in present-day Yunnan) had a close
relationship with the ox, an important emblem of production
and wealth. Apart from this, it was also an animal used in
sacrifices to the gods. This piece reveals characteristics of the
ancient culture of the Dian. (Su Qiang)

66

Gold-plated Heavenly King

Tang (618–907)
Height 71 cm, Width 27 cm

This Buddhist guardian figure of a Heavenly
King is made from bronze and, apart from its
hair, is gold plated. Its staring eyes and gaping
mouth revealing its teeth give it an imposing
and indignant look. It has fiery hair, and an
armour-clad body engraved with lively and
fluent lines. The shoulder parts are in the form
of dragon heads and there is an animal head
design on the stomach section. Its right hand
is on its hip, its left raised in the air. Trampled
below its feet are two small demons, both vivid
and lifelike, giving the whole an enthusiastic
feel. (Su Qiang)

68

Mirror with gold and silver designs of
feathered figures, flowers and birds

Tang (618–907)

Diameter 36.2 cm

*Excavated in Zhengzhou,
Henan Province*

67

Mirror with inlaid shell
design of scholars feasting
and playing music

Tang (618–907)

Diameter 23.9 cm

*Excavated in 1955 from Luoyang,
Henan Province*

70

Zheng He bell

Ming (1368–1644)

Height 83 cm,
Diameter at mouth 49 cm,
Thickness 2 cm

69

Mirror with pattern of playing ball

Song (960–1279)

Diameter 10.6 cm,
Thickness 0.6 cm

The game shown here is the world's earliest example of football and is first seen in the ancient city of Linzi in the state of Qi (in present-day Shandong Province) in the Spring and Autumn and Warring States periods, showing it to be a popular locally developed sport. The sport consisted of both a competitive kicking game and, by the Tang and Song periods, a professional performance of skill in which the leather ball was filled with air rather than feathers as was originally done. Women also became adept. This mirror shows high-relief design of both men and women playing the game. (Sheng Weiren)

POTTERY

The invention of pottery is a significant step in the development of human civilization, bringing in a new era in which mankind started to exploit and transform nature. Chinese ceramics are renowned throughout the world for their long history, great variety, artistic worth and exquisite technique. They are an outstanding and significant part of China's cultural heritage.

The earliest pottery is found in the Neolithic period, both moulded and wheel-turned, with decorative motifs painted on the smooth body using natural pigments. Painted pottery of this period has been found at sites of the Yangshao, Majiayao, Dawenkou, Daxi and Qujialing cultures. Its diverse forms showcase the splendid art of these early cultures of China. The large painted pottery collection of the National Museum includes pieces of all the different types, of which the basins with human face and fish designs excavated at Banpo near Xian and the drums from Gansu Province are outstanding representatives.

The variety proliferated from the Western Zhou. Apart from household utensils, we see tiles and bricks, pottery figurines and funeral objects. In the Warring States and Qin periods, it became the custom to bury the dead with pottery models of everyday objects that led to a growth in pottery manufacture. The National Museum's collection includes the exquisite and realistic pottery soldiers and horses from the First Emperor's tomb and the *Red-painted animal handle square flask* from Yan Di, near Beijing. The latter is an imitation of a contemporary bronze ritual vessel with strong colour that captures both the dignity of the bronze as well as its form and structure.

In the Han period there was great progress in the selection and mixing of the clay to create both chalky and sand-mixed wares, which enabled the production of gigantic food and water storage vessels. Their decorative motifs are coloured, both pleasing to the eye and showing considerable artistic value. The pottery boat of the Eastern Han in the Museum's collection is a realistic scale model of a contemporary boat in its composition and form and is therefore extremely important for studying Chinese shipping history as well as being an outstanding representative of Eastern Han pottery art. The figurines from this period are also of a high standard and many possess admirable liveliness. The Eastern Han storytellers with their caricatured expressions but lifelike modelling possess great artistic value.

Polychrome wares, known as *sancai* in Chinese or tricolour, used coloured lead glazes fired at a low temperature, with yellow, dark grey and green predominating. In the Tang period there was more variation in the colours, and the glazers experimented by mixing glazes to form a mottled effect and letting the glazes run and mix together. Tang polychrome wares are bright and show flowing lines. The polychrome camel with a troupe of musicians on its back is an outstanding representative piece of the High Tang period, lofty in form with clearly demarcated colours, which reveals the style of the flourishing Tang society. Tang polychromes are popular and influential throughout the world, loved by peoples from all countries. (Yu Lu)

72

Pot with hermaphrodite naked figure

Neolithic, Majiayao Culture (3200–2000 bc)

Height 33.4 cm

Excavated in 1974 from Liuwan, Leduxian, Qinghai Province

71

Painted pottery drum

Neolithic, Majiayao Culture (3200–2000 BC)

Length 36.9 cm, Diameter of face 29.2 cm, Diameter of handle 9.3 cm

Excavated in 1986 from Leshanping, Lanzhou, Gansu Province

73

Jar showing a stork with a fish and a stone axe

Neolithic, Yangshao Culture (5000–3000 bc)
Height 46.8 cm, Diameter at mouth 62.7 cm,
Diameter at base 20.1 cm
*Excavated in 1978 from Yancun, Linruxian,
Henan Province*

This belongs to the Yangshao Neolithic Culture, the white
pigment having been pressed on to form the pictures of a
stork, fish and stone axe, the stork's eye, the fish and sections
of the axe depicted with black outlines. The stork stands
upright holding a large fish in its mouth, while to the right is
a stone axe bound to a wooden handle. The paint is thick and
congealed. The motif reflects the hunting and fishing lifestyle of
the peoples of this time and place, and it is a rare and valuable
example of painted pottery from this early period. (Yu Lu)

74

Hawk-shaped cauldron

Neolithic, Yangshao Culture (5000–3000 BC)
Height 36 cm
Excavated in 1958 from Taipingzhuang, Huaxian, Shaanxi Province

This pottery cauldron is a simple design yet has both power and grandeur. Its solid belly is formed by the hawk's plump chest with the mouth opening on the hawk's back. The hawk has a hooked beak and round eyes, and the body is undecorated. The paired wings circle round the back and the legs of the cauldron are formed from the hawk's legs and its tail, giving it stability. (Yu Lu)

75

Basin with design of dancers

Neolithic, Majiayao Culture (3200–2000 BC)
Height 14 cm, Diameter at mouth 28 cm
*Excavated in 1973 from Sunjiazhai,
Datong County, Qinghai Province*

This piece is made from fine red clay with a restrained mouth, rolled lip and slightly convex belly tapering to a small circular base. It has been decorated with black paint. The outside has a simple design of three lines, but on the inside similar lines frame a painting of three groups of dancers. Each group comprises five figures holding hands. Their hair is braided and a decoration hangs from their body. The braid and decoration fall on different sides of each figure, giving a sense of movement to the group. The outer arm of the outer two figures of each group is painted with two lines, perhaps to express the swaying of their arms during the dance.

A wonderful feature of this bowl is that, when it is full of water, the ripples of the water imbue the painted figures with a sense of movement, so that they appear to be dancing. Many scholars have studied this scene, offering different interpretations. Some suggest that it is a hunting dance, some a religious dance, others a ceremonial dance, yet others hypothesize that the aim of the dance is for a bumper harvest. (Yu Lu)

76

Basin with a fish pattern
with a human face

Neolithic, Yangshao Culture (5000–4000 BC)
Height 16.5 cm, Diameter at mouth 39.5 cm
Excavated in 1955 from Banpo, Xian,
Shaanxi Province

This is a treasure of the Neolithic. Made from fine red clay it has a wide lip and, on the inside, black painted decorations of two opposing faces and two fish. The faces are circular with arch-shaped black areas on the forehead, on the right side, possibly a local facial tattoo tradition. The straight nose and the eyes depicted by thin straight lines give it a serene appearance. The open mouth is formed of the heads of two fish, their bodies extending either side of the face, and the ears are also depicted as small fish, creating a peculiar merman-like form. It shows great imagination. On its head is a triangular-shaped object, possibly a depiction of hair, but also with the appearance of the fin of a fish.

Many of the pottery basins found at Banpo have a fish and net design, which probably have both an economic and a totemic significance. The Banpo people lived in terraced settlements in a river valley, dependant on agriculture but with hunting and fishing as a supplement. The unusual headdress most probably represents that worn during a religious ceremony, where the human was believed to transform into the spirit of the god – a fish god – hence the fish fin hat. It suggests that the people of Banpo used fish as a totem. (Yu Lu)

77

Red-painted animal handle square flask

Warring States (475–221 bc)

Height 70 cm, Diameter at mouth 20 cm

Excavated in 1957 from Warring State tomb at Songyuancun, Changping District, Beijing

78

Tomb soldier of the First Emperor

Qin (221–206 bc)

Height 190 cm

Excavated in 1974 from pit No. 1, tomb of Qin Shihuangdi, Lingtong, Shaanxi Province

79

Painted tomb figurine of a long-sleeved female dancer

Western Han (202 bc – ad 8)

Height 49 cm

Excavated in 1954 from Baijiakou, Xian, Shaanxi Province

80

Tomb figurine of a storyteller

Eastern Han (25–220)
Height 55 cm
*Excavated in 1957 from tomb No. 3,
Tianhuishan, Chengdu, Sichuan Province*

This piece was discovered in the central part of the corridor of the sandstone tomb. It is an unusual piece among tomb figurines. It was made in reddish clay from a combination of casting and hand moulding. The figure wears a kerchief coiled around his head and knotted at the front. His torso is naked showing his drooping belly and he wears bracelets on both arms, the one on the left made of pearls. His left arm is curled around a circular drum, 11.5 cm in diameter. The 19-cm-long drumstick is in his raised right hand, as if he is about to

beat the drum. He wears wide trousers but his feet are bare, and the sole of his right foot is raised up and facing out. The circumference of his bent left leg is 24.5 cm. He raises his head, his eyes crinkled and forehead creased with laughter. This is a joyous piece, filled with humour and spirit, bringing to life a performing artist of 2000 years ago. We can see him as an ancestor of today's performers. This figurine tells us that storytelling thrived in the Han period and that sculptural art had reached a comparatively high level. (Xi Yuying)

81

Green glazed house

Eastern Han (25–220)

Height 152.3 cm

*Excavated in 1956 from Gaotangxian,
Liaocheng, Shandong Province*

82

Boat

Eastern Han (25–220)

Height 16 cm, Length 54 cm

*Excavated in 1955 from tomb No. 5080,
Xianlielu, eastern suburbs of Guangdong*

83

Painted tomb figurine of a lute player

Northern Qi (550–577)
Height 28.2 cm
Excavated in 1973 from Shedihuiluo tomb, Shouyangxian, Shanxi

In total, 120 figurines of different forms were excavated from this tomb, all made of grey pottery using moulds and, on several, the colouring has remained bright. There were two lute players with basically the same figure: this is one of them. He wears a red hat, a round-necked shirt with long white sleeves with wide openings and, over it, a red jacket, long sleeves reaching to his knees, the neckline, sleeves and bottom hem all being decorated with a broad red band. It is tied at the waist with a belt, which sticks out on the left side. He wears long and wide white trousers – both ends of the belt hang down at the front – and round shoes. He has long eyebrows and narrow eyes; his lips are painted with vermillion and he holds a black-outlined five-stringed lute – a *pipa*. His left hand holds its neck and the thumb of his right hand is pointed up in the act of plucking the string. The modelling of all the features is accurate, portraying a pretty lute-playing youth who is concentrating entirely on his music. (Xi Yuying)

85

Tomb figure of a horsewoman

Sui (561–618)

Height 38 cm, Width 30 cm

Excavated in 1956 from Boyushan,
Wuhan, Hubei Province

84

Tomb figurine showing warrior
with braided beard and sword

Sui (561–618)

Height 99 cm

Excavated in 1956 from tomb No. 241 at
Zhoujiadawan, Wuhan, Hubei Province

87

Painted tomb figurine of
woman with double bun

Tang (618–907)

Height 31.5 cm

86

Painted and gilded tomb figurine
showing ceremonial guard

Tang (618–907)

Height 70 cm

*Excavated in 1971 from tomb at Zhengrentai,
Liquanxian, Shaanxi Province*

88

Painted tomb figurine of a saddle horse and groom

Tang (618–907)
Height of horse 40 cm,
Height of groom 36.8 cm

*Said to have been excavated from
Luoyang, Henan Province*

In the Tang the use of kaolin or china clay made for a very smooth white finish for objects such as these. The groom and horse were cast in separate moulds and then finished by hand. They were both originally painted but much has flaked away. The groom wears a kerchief on his head. His undershirt is white with half-length sleeves. Over it he wears a jacket with red lapels, which is gathered at the waist with a belt. The jacket has fallen off his left shoulder and the narrow sleeves are rolled up. His trousers are red and tucked into leggings and into his pointed-toed shoes. He is looking to his right with his mouth open as if calling, with his right arm holding the rein and his left arm extended back for balance. His front foot is planted firmly on the ground, and his back foot is raised with toe on the ground. He is leaning backwards and is pulling against the

horse. The horse's head is pulling down and away, his mouth is open, nostrils flared and ears pricked. His front left leg is raised high in the air and back legs are flexed as if resisting the rein. The horse's tackle and ornaments are complete, from his gorgeous saddle blanket, his bridle, saddle, stirrups, girth, small bells and tassels. His body is glazed a deep and light yellow.

The sculptor has succeeded in realizing a complex concept, that of a trainer fighting with his wild steed, and has given great realism to the piece even down to the folds of the trainer's clothes and the musculature of the horse. It has a vivacity which is rare among Tang-period tomb figurines. (Jiang Yutao)

90

Polychrome glazed tomb figurines of a troupe of musicians on horseback

Tang (618–907)

Average Height 35 cm, Average Length 30 cm

Excavated in 1972 from the tomb of Li Zhen, Luquanxian, Shaanxi Province

89

Tomb figurines showing a troupe of kneeling musicians

Tang (618–907)

Average Height 11cm

Excavated in 1955 from the tomb of Wei Jiong, eastern suburbs of Guangzhou, Guangdong Province

92

Painted tomb figurine of
merchant from the regions
west of China holding a pot

Tang (618–907)
Height 27 cm
Excavated from Xian, Shaanxi Province

91

Painted tomb figurine of a woman
bent over in sleep

Tang (618–907)
Height 11 cm
*Excavated in 1954 from the tomb of Wang Chen, in
the eastern suburbs of Changzhi, Shanxi Province*

93

Polychrome glazed tomb figurine
of a woman holding a tray

Tang (618–907)

Height 45.3 cm

*Excavated in 1957 from tomb at Xianyutinghui
tomb, Xian, Shaanxi Province*

94

Polychrome glazed tomb
figurine of a seated woman

Tang (618–907)

Height 28.7 cm

*Excavated in 1953 from Xian,
Shaanxi province*

95

Blue glazed tomb figurine of a woman in foreigners' dress

Tang (618–907)

Height 25 cm

Excavated in 1955 from tomb No. 337 at Shilipu, Xian, Shaanxi Province

This figurine was made in a mould using kaolin giving a clean white result. She wears a small hat decorated with a cloud design and with a high crown of white felt. Her blue gown is not Chinese dress, with its narrow sleeves and wide brown lapels with left crossing right – Chinese clothes cross the other way. It is tied at the waist with a narrow belt. Below she wears long white trousers and blue shoes with turned-up pointed toes.

Her right arm is held in front of her chest with her hand in a fist, and her left arm hangs down by her side with her hand inside the sleeve. This is a young lady dressed in the so-called 'foreigner's dress', fashionable among the Tang elite women at this time.

Tang women not only wore men's clothes, but also imitated the fashion of other foreigners, both clothes and hats. Before the Tang, these were mainly the clothes of the nomadic peoples from the north-western steppe, who wore clothes made of fur and felt and tall pointed hats with flaps which could be folded down to protect their ears. (Xi Yuying)

96

Tomb figurine showing a foreigner on a green glazed camel

Tang (618–907)

Height of figure 41.6 cm,
Height of camel 113 cm, Length 88.7 cm

*Excavated in 1956 from Dugusijing tomb,
Xian, Shaanxi Province*

97

Streaked glaze tomb figurine of a mounted hunter

Tang (618–907)

Height 37 cm, Length of horse 29 cm

*Excavated in 1975 from Qianxian,
Shaanxi Province*

99

Polychrome glazed tomb figurine on seated camel

Tang (618–907)

Height 39.4 cm, Length 47 cm

Excavated in 1957 from Xianyutinghui tomb, Xian, Shaanxi Province

98

Polychrome glazed horse tomb figurine

Tang (618–907)

Height 54 cm, Length 54 cm

Excavated in 1957 from Xianyutinghui tomb, Xian, Shaanxi Province

100

Polychrome glazed tomb figurine of a troupe of musicians on a camel

Tang (618–907)

Height 67 cm, Length 50 cm, Width 20 cm

Excavated in 1957 from Xianyutinghui tomb, Xian, Shaanxi Province

Made of kaolin, this piece has a smooth, hard glaze. The camel is tall with raised head and robust physique. It is white apart from its mane and other hair, which is deep yellow. Over its humps is an oval, green, yellow and blue saddle blanket; over that, a flat platform; and then a green-edged rug with blue, yellow, green and white stripes in a white pearl border. Five musicians are on the platform; three are foreigners from countries west of China, with wide cheekbones, deep-set eyes, large hooked noses, sideburns and beards. The one seated at the front left, holding a lute, wears a blue jacket with yellow lapels and white boots with upturned pointed toes. Behind him sits a Chinese-looking figure in a long-sleeved round-collared green jacket, playing a wind instrument. The two percussionists on the camel's right side are dressed in brown. The singer standing in their midst wears a long-sleeved green-belted tunic with round collar, his right arm raised, his left arm hanging with his hand hidden in the sleeve. The piece gives a realistic idea of the life of a musical troupe with both Chinese and foreign members. (Jiang Yutao)

101

**Black and polychrome
glazed horse tomb figurine**

Tang (618–907)
Height 67.2 cm, Length 78.2 cm
*Excavated in 1972 from Guanlin,
Luoyang, Henan Province*

This piece is made from kaolin using a mould. This blue-black glaze is rarely seen because it is unstable at the high firing temperatures then used. The horse's face, mane and tail are white. Its mane is neatly trimmed, its tail wrapped and its tack complete: a white-coloured bridle, reins marked with a square pattern, saddle covered with hanging green silk knotted on each side, an oval brown-glazed saddle blanket with white dotted design and a white girth. The glaze is evenly distributed, bright and smooth. The horse stands proudly on all four feet, hoofs white as the snow; he has the qualities of a top-quality horse from the western regions. In modelling and glaze this excellent example of polychrome ware shows the crystallization of the combined arts of sculpture and pottery. (Wang Wei)

103

Tomb figurine of a flautist

Jin (1115–1234)

Height 38.5 cm

Excavated in 1973 from Jin tomb at Xifengcun, Jiaozuo, Henan Province

102

Tomb figurine of a clapperboard player

Jin (1115–1234)

Height 36.5 cm

Excavated in 1973 from Jin tomb at Xifengcun, Jiaozuo, Henan Province

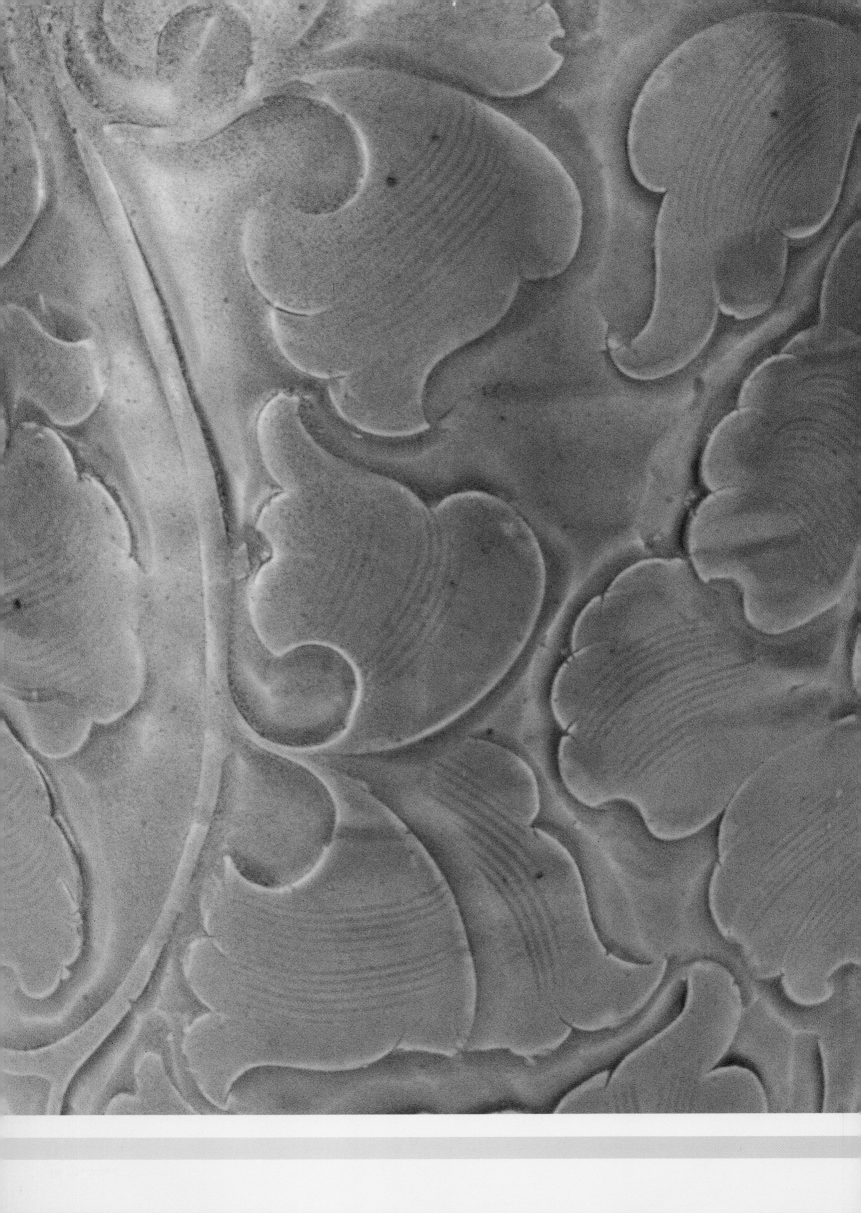

PORCELAIN

Chinese ceramics, with their long history, offer a reflection of Chinese history, from their invention, development and many transformations. Not only do they showcase technological advances but also the changes and developments in society and in the material and spiritual life of the Chinese people.

Although we see stone wares in China 3000 years ago during the Shang period, the firing process and materials were not mature enough at this time to produce porcelain. High-fired stone wares started to be produced in the Eastern Han period.

Porcelains, made from kaolin and feldspar fired at a temperature of between 1250 °C and 1450 °C to produce very hard and thin ceramics, appear in the Tang, represented by the green-glazed celadon or Yue wares produced in the south, described as 'like ice and jade', and the white wares of the north – 'like silver and snow'.

Porcelains show great variety and excellence in the Song period. The five major wares were Ru, Ding, Guan, Ge and Jun, along with the products of the kilns of Yaozhou in the north, and Longquan and Jingdezhen in the south. Each type had distinguishing features resulting from differences in the firing process and each piece is a unique work of art.

From the Yuan to the Qing periods production prospered, with the Jingdezhen kilns in Jiangxi Province becoming the centre of production for the whole country, and being representative of Chinese porcelain manufacture. Imperial kilns were established early in the Ming period to produce pieces for use in the imperial palace and this institution continued into later times.

The Museum's collection comprises several thousand pieces which cover the historical development of porcelain from the Eastern Han all the way through to the Qing. Some pieces have been excavated from important tombs, archaeological sites and Buddhist pagodas. Those from tombs which are dated or which contain an inscription giving the era provide the basis for classification by periods based on their distinctive features.

Examples are the Northern dynasties lotus-patterned *zun* vase from the Feng family tombs in Hebei, and the Yue kiln *mise* ('secret colour') bowl from the late Tang found at Famen Temple Pagoda, Shaanxi Province.

The Museum's collection of renowned Song-period Ru, Guan, Jun, Longquan and Yaozhou wares showcases the expertise involved in the manufacture of porcelains.

The largest part of the Museum's collection is that of wares from the Jingdezhen kilns from the Ming and Qing periods. Their quality is superb. Around the world, the Ming and Qing blue-and-white wares are the most famous and considered the most characteristic of China. The Museum holds important representative Ming-period pieces.

The Museum holds collections of overglaze enamels of the Ming and Qing, including polychrome and *famille rose* wares. The most valuable are the *cloisonné* enamel from the Qing period, which represent the pinnacle of Chinese glazing techniques. During the reign of the Qing emperor Qianlong relatively few enamels of fine quality were produced but they are renowned as representing the apex of Qing porcelain manufacture as well as showing the intermingling of Chinese and Western culture in the 18th century.

Monochrome ware from Jingdezhen also reached a level of perfection in this period, for example, in the Ming, the white glaze of the Yongle period, the red glaze of the Xuande period, the yellow glaze of the Hongliang period. In the Qing we see the great treasures of the Kangxi-period *sang de boeuf* and kidney-bean-red wares.

The Museum has porcelains representative of all periods, which provide a snapshot showing the development of porcelain from earliest times and which reflect the fascination of the brilliant art of Chinese porcelain. (Geng Dongsheng)

104

Green glazed candlestick in form of a ram

Three Kingdoms, Wu (222–280)
Height 24.9 cm, Length 31.7 cm
*Excavated in 1958 from Wu tomb
on Beijinglu, Nanjing, Jiangsu Province*

This candlestick is in the form of a ram, head high and mouth open with his horns curling around his ears. The round hole in his forehead is for inserting a candle. He has a strong, stout body with long lines depicting hair on his back and shoulders and wings on the sides of his belly. The grey-green glaze has a slight yellowish tinge.

In ancient times the Chinese character for ram, 'yang', was the same as that for 'xiang', which is the word for luck, so the ram was seen as an auspicious animal and used in burials to avert bad fortune. This candlestick has an ingenious design with interesting decoration and is a rare treasure of Eastern Wu green wares from the Three Kingdoms period.
(Yu Wenrong)

105

**Green glazed pot with figures
in a building and a barn**

Western Jin (265–316)

Height 43.2 cm, Diameter at base 16.5 cm

Excavated from Shaoxing, Zhejiang Province

106

Green glazed incense burner (with tray)

Western Jin (265–316)

Combined Height 19.5 cm

*Excavated in 1953 from tomb group No. 1,
Yixing, Zhejiang Province*

107

Green glazed vase covered with lotus designs

Northern Qi (550–577)

Height 63.6 cm, Diameter at mouth 19.4 cm, Diameter at foot 20.2 cm

Excavated in 1948 from Feng family tombs, Jingxian, Hebei Province

The vase has a flared mouth, long neck, sloping shoulder, long round belly, high ring foot and a lid. There are two small bridge-shaped handles on the neck and a further six ring handles on the shoulder. The decoration comprises 13 registers, all formed of lotus petals apart from the flower appliqués and the stamped round animal designs on the neck. The lid is formed of double-layered lotus petals with a knob on top and double lotus petals sticking up around the edge. The top part of the belly is covered with three registers of lotus petals and the lower part has a double layer of impressed petal designs. The modelling of the decoration is meticulous and well balanced between the upper and lower parts. The lotus is a Buddhist symbol to represent purity, used here to take care of the spirit of the deceased.

This is a large piece, stately and imposing, with a smooth green glaze. It is one of the very few ceramics extant from the Northern Qi period and is an unrivalled piece for the study of ceramic production and design in the Northern dynasties period. (Yu Wenrong)

108

White glazed double dragon, double-bellied vase

Sui (581–618)

Height 19 cm, Diameter at mouth 4.6 cm

Excavated in 1957 from Li Jingxun's tomb, Xian, Shaanxi Province

109

Marbled ware pillow

Tang (618–907)

Height 7.7 cm, Length 14.7 cm, Width 10 cm

Excavated in 1956 from Tang tomb, Liujiaqu, Shanxian, Henan Province

110

Patterned glazed pot

Tang (618–907)

Height 30.9 cm,
Diameter at mouth 6–10.6 cm,
Diameter at base 9.1 cm

*Excavated in 1956 from a Tang tomb,
Liujiaqu, Shanxian, Henan Province*

111

Mise olive green bowl

Tang (618–907)

Height 4.6 cm,
Diameter at mouth 24.8 cm

*Excavated in 1987 from the underground
treasure pit at Famen Temple Pagoda, Fufeng,
Shaanxi Province*

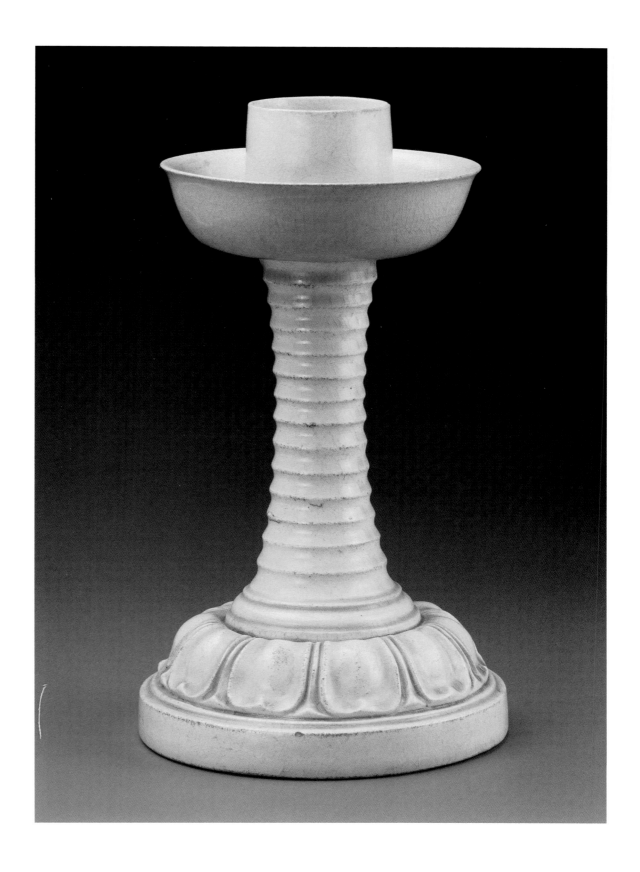

112

White glazed lamp stand on a lotus base

Tang (618–907)

Height 30.4 cm,
Diameter at mouth 6.5 cm,
Diameter at base 17.3 cm

*Excavated in 1957 from Tang tomb,
Houchuan, Shanxian, Henan Province*

The lamp stand consists of the lamp tray, a long stem and the foot. The tray is in the form of a shallow bowl with a small cup in the centre, raised above the rim of the bowl. The stem takes the form of a thin pillar with an even, ridged design. The foot resembles the base of a pillar covered with clearly modelled high-relief lotus petals with a plain base below. This is a consummate piece of hand carving with a pure white glaze that has a smooth and lustrous gloss. It is an extremely rare and superb piece of Tang white ware. (Yu Wenrong)

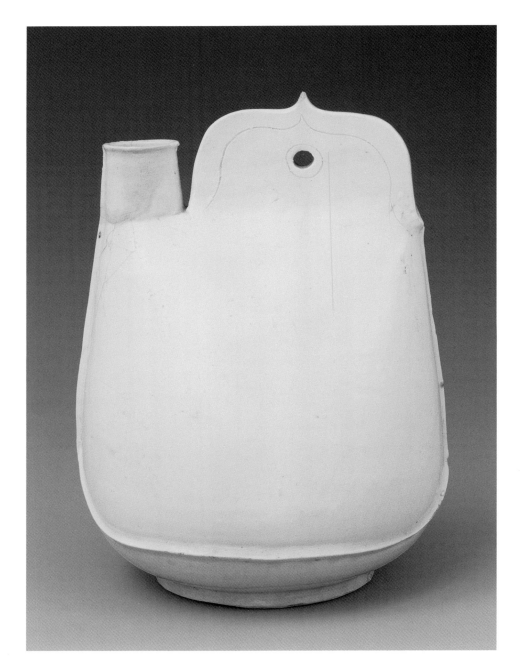

113
White glazed stirrup flask

Five Dynasties (907–960)

Height 26.3 cm

Excavated in 1953 from Dagong Liao tombs at Chifeng, Inner Mongolian Autonomous Region

114

Ru ware green glazed washing bowl

Northern Song (960–1127)

Height 5.2 cm,
Diameter at mouth 16.7 cm,
Diameter at foot 13.1 cm

115

Ding ware white glazed lotus pattern bowl

Northern Song (960–1127)

Height 15.5 cm,
Diameter at mouth 31.8 cm,
Diameter at foot 15.3 cm

116

Jun ware purple glazed flower pot

Northern Song (960–1127)

*Height 14.4 cm, Diameter at widest
point of mouth 24 cm, Diameter at
widest point of foot 13 cm*

117

Yaozhou ware green glazed
turnip-pattern wine vessel

Northern Song (960–1127)

Height 24.2 cm,
Diameter at mouth 5 cm,
Diameter at foot 6.5 cm

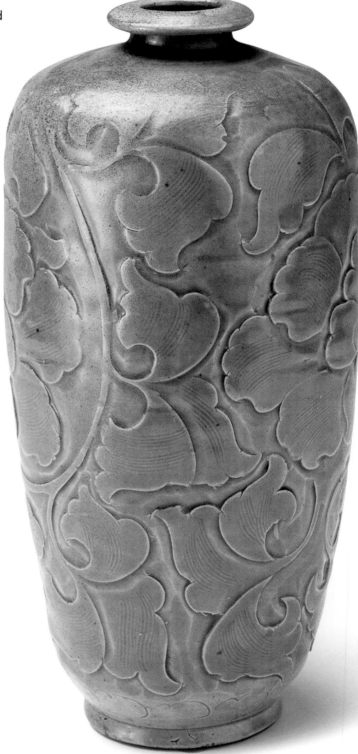

118

Yaozhou ware green glazed
incised flower decoration
Go case

Northern Song (960–1127)

Height 8.4 cm, Diameter 11.6 cm

119

Chaozhou ware green-white glazed Buddha

Northern Song (960–1127)
Height 31 cm, Base 10.1 cm

120

Jingdezhen ware green-white glazed washing bowl and ewer

Southern Song (1127–1279)

Height of flagon 23.2 cm,
Height of bowl 20.9 cm

Excavated in 1983 from Southern Song tomb at Jiangdengyunshan, Jiangsu Province

121

Guan ware small box

Southern Song (1127–1279)

Height 9.9 cm, Diameter at mouth
16.8 cm, Diameter at foot 18.6 cm

122

Guan ware vase with
pierced handles

Southern Song (1127–1279)

Height 23 cm, Greatest dimensions of
mouth 8.3 x 6.6 cm,

Diameter at foot 9.7 x 8.1 cm

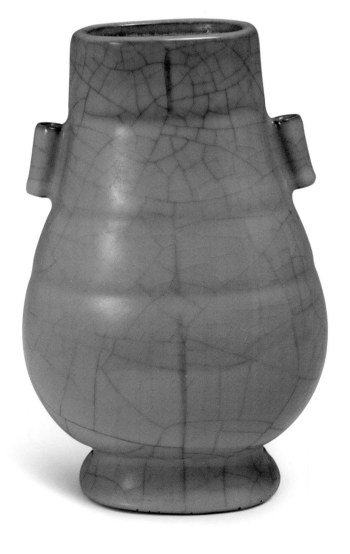

123

Longquan ware green glazed vase with pierced handles

Southern Song (1127–1279)

Height 33.3 cm, Diameter at mouth 11.1 cm, Diameter at foot 12.7 cm

124

White glazed long-necked ewer with door-knocker design

Southern Song (1127–1279)

Height 25 cm, Diameter at mouth 7.5 cm, Diameter at foot 8 cm

Found in 2003 in the sea at Yangjiang, Guangdong Province

126

Ding ware patterned pillow

Jin (1115–1234)

Height 13.1 cm, Length 23.2 cm,
Width 19.7 cm

125

Cizhou ware pillow
with lotus design in
black on white slip

Jin (1115–1234)

Height 21.2 cm

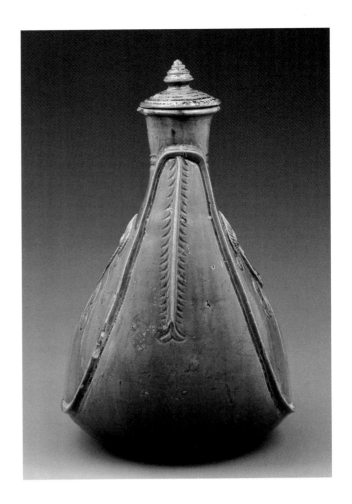

127

Green glazed dragon and line design stirrup cup

Liao (907–1125)

Height 28.5 cm, Diameter at mouth 5.5 cm,
Diameter at base 10.5 cm

128

Lingwu ware dark glaze floral-pattern incised and carved flat pot

Western Xia (Tangut) (1032–1227)

Height 33.3 cm, Diameter at mouth 9 cm

129

Ge ware fish ear censer

Yuan (1271–1368)
Height 8.7 cm,
Diameter at mouth 11.9 cm,
Diameter of base 17.2 cm

This is an object for display but its origins can be traced to the *gui* bronze food vessels of the Shang and Zhou periods, although this porcelain version is much more delicate, refined and artistic. It has a low body with a broad belly and fish-shaped handles on either side, restrained yet dignified. The body is covered with a greenish-grey glaze densely covered with crackle decoration emulating a design fashionable in ancient China.

Ge wares are among the finest porcelains in the history of Chinese ceramics, and we know from historical sources that they were produced in the Longquan area of Zhejiang Province. Yet, despite 50 years of extensive excavation in this area, archaeologists have still failed to find the location of the Ge ware kilns. (Zhang Yan)

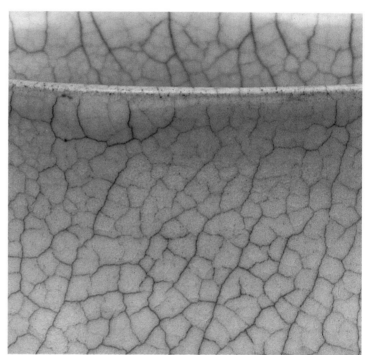

130

Jingdezhen blue-and-white
paired phoenix vase

Yuan (1271–1368)

Height 25.8 cm, Diameter at mouth 7.2 cm,
Diameter at foot 7.4 cm

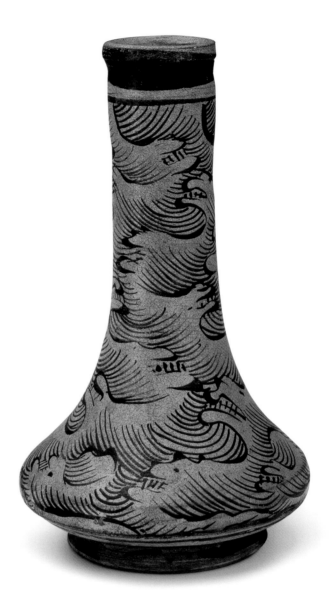

131

Jizhou ware grey glaze long-necked flask

Yuan (1271–1368)

Height 13.4 cm,
Diameter at mouth 2.6 cm

132

Jun ware blue glaze appliqué vase with animal head, two ears and linked flower-pattern mouth

Yuan (1271–1368)

Height 63.2 cm,
Diameter at mouth 15.2 cm,
Diameter at foot 17.5 cm

Excavated in 1972 from Yuan period site at Xinjiekou, Xichengqu, Beijing

With a mouth in the shape of a five-petalled flower, this vase has a long neck and short curved shoulder leading to the belly. Ram-shaped handles link the neck and shoulder and the body is decorated with a raised animal head roundel design with the character for king on its head. The vase sits on a base with five openings, but the pieces are joined and cannot be separated. The base is decorated with an animal head relief around its neck. The sky blue glaze is generous and smooth, with purple blotches left from a reduction of the glaze on the mouth, on the belly and decorating the base. The ochre-red colour on the base is evidence of oxidization during firing. The piece shows the beauty and vigour of Yuan-period porcelains. Vase and base sets are common among Longquan wares from the Yuan period, but rare among Jun wares. Two pieces were excavated at this site but were already badly broken and have been restored. (Zhang Yan)

133

Cizhou ware vase showing a child playing

Yuan (1271–1368)
Height 30.6 cm, Diameter at mouth 18.5 cm,
Diameter at belly 30.8 cm, Diameter at base 12.5 cm
Found in 1998 in the sea at Suizhong, Liaoning Province

The body of the vase bears a picture of a child
playing among flowers, with a plump face, wearing
a patterned Chinese bib and holding a stem of leaves
in both hands; he is surrounded by peonies and
chrysanthemums. This design was very popular. This
piece was among 600 porcelains discovered in 1995 in
a shipwreck off the coast of Liaoning at Suizhong: over
20 were of this type. From the Tang and Song periods
the Cizhou kilns were the most flourishing in northern
China. The clay quality is not so high but the black slip
design on a white slip base covered with a transparent
glaze results in a striking effect. (Zhang Yan)

134

Blue-and-white dragon and phoenix three-footed censer

Hongwu reign period (1368–1398), Ming
Height 37.5 cm, Diameter at mouth 27.5 cm

135

Underglazed red vase with design of coiled chrysanthemums

Hongwu reign period (1368–1398), Ming
Height 32.1 cm, Diameter at mouth 8.3 cm,
Diameter at base 11.9 cm

136
Blue-and-white vase with design of bamboo, rocks, plantains and plum blossom

Yongle reign period (1403–1424), Ming

Height 41 cm, Diameter at mouth 5.5 cm, Diameter at base 12.2 cm

137
Blue-and-white ewer with plants and fruit design

Yongle reign period (1403–1424), Ming

Height 26.1, Diameter at mouth 6.4 cm, Diameter at base 9.8 cm

138

White pot with hidden lotus branch design

Yongle reign period (1403–1424), Ming

Height 9.4 cm, Diameter at mouth 10.3 cm,
Diameter at foot 14.3 cm

139

Blue-and-white stem foot cup with dragon in sea design

Xuande reign period (1426–1435), Ming

Height 18 cm, Diameter at mouth 15.7 cm,
Diameter at foot 7.8 cm

140

Red glazed plate

Xuande reign period (1426–1435), Ming

Height 4.4 cm, Diameter at mouth 20 cm,
Diameter at base 12.7 cm

141

Overglazed enamel *doucai* pot with butterfly design

Chenghua reign period (1465–1487), Ming

Height 9.3 cm, Diameter at mouth 7.4 cm,
Diameter at foot 9.4 cm

142

Overglazed enamel *wucai* pot with lid
with design of fish among aquatic plants

Jiajing reign period (1522–1566), Ming

Height 46 cm, Diameter at mouth 19.8 cm,
Diameter at foot 24.8 cm

*Excavated in 1955 from the eastern
suburbs of Beijing*

The short neck leads to a full body that tapers down gradually
to the base. The lid is in the shape of heaven and earth, with
a precious pearl-shaped knob. The harmonious and peaceful
design of fish swimming, feeding and frolicking among
aquatic grasses, reeds, lotus and duckweed is achieved using
underglaze blue with overglazed enamel decoration. This
design transmutes into supplementary designs of lotus petals,
banana leaves, pearl necklaces and the eight treasures. The

base has an inscription in blue of six Chinese characters in two
lines in regular (*kai*) script, 'Made in the Jia jing reign period of
the Great Ming [dynasty]'.

Overglazed enamel decorated *wucai* wares are among the
most famous porcelains of the Ming and Qing period. This large
piece with its painting in classical style and bright colours is a
masterpiece of its type from the Jia jing reign period. (Geng
Dongsheng)

143

Blue-and-white pot showing paired dragons playing with a pearl

Longqing reign period (1567–1572), Ming
Height 35.6 cm, Diameter at mouth 69 cm,
Diameter at base 52.5 cm

144

Overglazed enamel *wucai* vase with design of auspicious animals and sunflowers

Wanli reign period (1573–1620), Ming
Height 36.5 cm, Diameter at mouth 12.5 cm,
Diameter at foot 11.3 cm

145

Swatow ware white glazed seated Buddha

Wanli reign period (1573–1620), Ming
Height 62.6 and 25.2 cm, Base 25.4 x 21 cm

Sakyamuni Buddha is seated on a lotus platform, with his robe draped over his left shoulder and his right shoulder bare, revealing a Buddhist swastika symbol on his chest. The piece is white-glazed with a yellow tinye, with tiny flakes and ash-grey marks. Three characters to one side of the hole on the base read 'Kaiyuan Monastery'. On the other side are 13 characters in two lines reading 'Great Ming [dynasty], Wanli 52nd year Zhangzhou (Swatow) Prefecture, East Creek Village'. The characters are in regular (*kai*) script with the groves filled with gold.

This Buddha, with his serene composure and succinct yet mellow lines, is representative of the products of the Swatow kilns in the Ming period. (Geng Dongsheng)

146

**Blue-and-white pot with
multiple longevity characters**

Wanli reign period (1573–1620), Ming

Height 49 cm, Diameter at mouth 22.9 cm,
Diameter at foot 26 cm

148

Yellow *cloisonné* enamel
bowl with peonies

Kangxi reign period (1662–1722), Qing

Height 7.6 cm, Diameter at mouth 15.6 cm,
Diameter at foot 6.1 cm

147

Overglaze enamel *doucai* vase
with pheasant and peony

Kangxi reign period (1662–1722), Qing

Height 25.5 cm, Diameter at mouth 59 cm,
Diameter at foot 50 cm

149

Sky-blue pot with chrysanthemum petal design

Kangxi reign period (1662–1722), Qing

Height 17.3 cm, Diameter at mouth 19.1 cm, Diameter at foot 15.8 cm

150

Famille rose overglaze enamel hexagonal bowl with flowers and plants

Yongzheng reign period (1723–1735), Qing

Height 8.9 cm, Diameter at mouth 10.2 cm, Diameter at foot 9.6 cm

151

Overglazed enamel *doucai*
vase with lotus pattern

Yongzheng reign period (1723–1735), Qing

Height 28.6 cm, Diameter at mouth 4.8 cm,
Diameter at foot 10.1 cm

152

Famille rose overglaze enamel vase with open work dragon design

Qianlong reign period (1736–1795), Qing

Height 30.3 cm, Diameter at mouth 8.5 cm, Diameter at foot 10.5 cm

153

Indigo glazed double-swallow-handled pot with designs of coiling peonies outlined in gold

Qianlong reign period (1736–1795), Qing
Height 31.2 cm, Diameter at mouth 24.8 cm,
Diameter at foot 22.3 cm

The straight mouth has a slightly out-turned lip and the short neck leads to a convex belly and circular foot. It is indigo glazed, with the belly bearing a design of coiling peony stems painted in gold. The neck also bears a gold-painted decoration of lotus petals while the bottom is decorated in pink. The white-glazed handles on the neck and shoulder are in the form of swallows. On the base are six characters in three lines in seal script reading 'Made in the Qianlong period of the Great Qing'.

This is a dignified piece with an even and pure indigo glaze of a gem-like colour and its gold decoration showing meticulous work by the craftsman; it is a top-quality royal product of the Qianlong period.

This was found in Haiyan hall of the old Qing palace of Yuanmingyuan, and it therefore has important historical interest. The National Museum has two pieces from this set. (Geng Dongsheng)

JADE

The National Museum has a rich collection of jades, dating from the Neolithic to the late imperial Ming and Qing. Those illustrated here are all quality products of their period and include both excavated and handed-down pieces.

China has been using jade since earliest times. Recent archaeological discoveries have confirmed that jade objects were produced in China over 8,000 years ago, but the initial use of jade objects can probably be placed even earlier to 10,000 years ago, and has remained an unbroken tradition to the present.

The use of jade is a thread running through the whole history of the Chinese people, deeply influential and a beacon of the best in civilization. Jade production in China can be divided into three historical stages based on the differences in modelling and function: a spiritual phase; a ritual phase; and a popular phase.

The spiritual phase can be placed mainly in the mid to late Neolithic, its common characteristic the use of jade in burials to entrust the deceased to the care of the gods. Jade was thus seen as a material that enabled communication between the world of humans and the world of spirits. Shown here are the Hongshan Culture jade dragon, famous as the first dragon of China, and the jade *cong* with a human mask design, among the best *cong* in China.

The ritual phase continued through the pre-Shang and Shang periods to the time of the Northern and Southern dynasties. Up to the Western Zhou, jade was used to reinforce royal power, and jade ceremonial weapons increase in number such as swords, hatchets and battle-axes, all representing military power. An example here is the animal face jade hatchet. Typical are the jades found at Anyang in the tomb of Fu Hao, the consort of the Shang king Wu Ding, in their great variety and exquisite decoration, such as the *Jade figure with protruding object*. The development and growth of the institution of wearing jade became representative of the Western Zhou period, alongside the use of jade in burials. In the Spring and Autumn and Warring States periods, wearing jade was symbol of rank and had become the main focus of jade development. New forms emerged constantly, some exceedingly delicate such as the cloud and dragon

jade ornament and the silver belt buckle with inlaid gold and jade animal head, both illustrated below. Based on Confucianism as the ritual system, at this time jades were assigned an ethical quality and there was a tendency towards personalizing them. They were used as a symbol of the prevailing belief in the moral authority of the nobles.

From the Qin dynasty in the late 3rd century BC to the 6th century AD, jades were used much less in ritual and more as popular objects. Decorative and practical jade artefacts started to appear. Han-period jades are the most typical, with jade decoration of swords and burial jades becoming prevalent in the Western Han, such as the *Jade burial suit with gold ties* illustrated below.

The main period for the use of popular jades was from the 6th century AD onwards. The use, decoration and forms of jades became completely secularized and their decoration became more realistic. Examples shown here are the gold-rimmed bowl from the Sui-period tomb of Li Jingxun and the Tang *Jade comb back decorated with crab apples*.

During the Liao, Song, Jin and Yuan periods, a rich variety of styles of jades from different traditions are seen. After the Song, jades became more archaic in form, and became very desirable and highly priced objects.

In the Ming and Qing, there was a great development in the production of popular jades, dominated by ornamental and everyday objects, with archaic jades and collectors' pieces also common. There was a meticulous system for the use of jades in the Ming imperial court with the use of elaborate decorations, such as lucky fruits, poetic verses, pine, bamboo and plum, happiness and good fortune characters, and other auspicious designs. Examples below are the *Double-phoenix-handle jade bowl* and the *Jade pot with longevity and good fortune design*. In the Qing, jades from the Qianlong period are the most refined with the greatest artistry and show the pinnacle of jade production in China. The *Jade bottle with plum blossom design* and *Double-linked bowls with six dragonfly handles with rings* are excellent examples. There was a tendency towards greater refinement, elaboration, secularization and jades for appreciation, many of them large and imposing. This was the golden age of Chinese jades.
(Zhang Runping)

154

Jade dragon

Neolithic, Hongshan Culture (6000–5000 BC)
Height 26.3 cm, Width 29.3 cm
Excavated in 1971 from Sanxingtalacun,
Ongniud Banner, Inner Mongolia Autonomous Region

Made of bluish-green jade, the dragon's body forms a C-shape. It has a long extended snout, protruding tear-shaped oval eyes, an upturned nose with a flat end and two nostrils, characteristic of a pig's snout. The mouth is depicted using fine lines. There is a regular network of fine lines on its forehead and jaw. Its mane extends along the back of its neck and spine and curls upwards like a long hook: it is 21 cm long. The mane is flat and thin with a shallow groove ground lengthways into its top and a pattern of fine lines. The edges and tip are ground to a blade-like sharpness. A hole pierces the middle of the body, 0.95 cm in diameter, and was used to suspend the dragon. The tails curls inwards and has a rounded end.

This piece is quite large, meticulously cut and exquisitely engraved with a very distinctive shape. While the dragon's facial features, a synthesis of several animals, are carved with care, its body is undecorated but powerful. The shape is simple and natural, yet possessing animation, and lacking legs, horns and scales the body resembles that of a large and powerful snake.

This is the earliest jade dragon discovered in China and dates from 5,000 years ago. With both material and spiritual force, it is a rare work of art, and has become famous as 'The First Dragon of China'. (Zhang Runping)

155

Jade cong with head of an immortal

Neolithic, Liangzhu Culture (5300–4200 BC)

Height 49.2 cm, Width at top 6.4 cm,
Width at bottom 5.6 cm

156

Jade phoenix

Neolithic, Shijiahe Culture (4700–4400 BC)

Widest Diameter 4.9 cm, Thickness 0.6–0.7 cm

*Excavated in 1955 from Luojiaboling site,
Tianmen, Hubei Province*

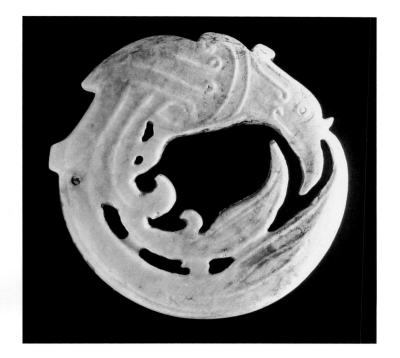

157

Animal face jade hatchet

Late Shang (1300–1046 BC)

Length 10.2 cm, Width 4.8 cm, Thickness 2.1 cm

Excavated in 1976 from the tomb of Fu Hao, Anyang, Henan Province

158

Jade food vessel with geometric design

Late Shang (1300–1046 BC)

Height 12.5 cm, Diameter at mouth 20.7 cm,

Diameter at foot 14.5 cm, Thickness 0.9 cm

Excavated in 1976 from the tomb of Fu Hao, Anyang, Henan Province

159

Jade dragon pendant

Late Shang (1300–1046 BC)

Height 5.6 cm, Length 8.1 cm

Excavated in 1976 from tomb of Fu Hao, Anyang, Henan Province

160

Jade tiger

Late Shang (1300–1046 BC)

Height 3.1 cm, Length 14 cm, Width 1.9 cm

Excavated in 1976 from tomb of Fu Hao, Anyang, Henan Province

161

'Sixin' stone ox

Late Shang (1300–1046 BC)

Height 14.5 cm, Length 25 cm, Width 11.5 cm

Excavated in 1976 from tomb of Fu Hao, Anyang, Henan Province

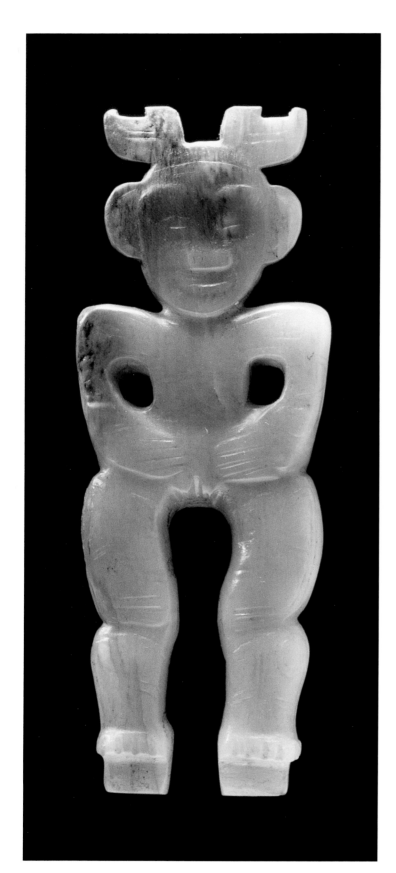

162

Jade matching figures

Late Shang (1300–1046 BC)

Height 12.5 cm, Width 4.5 cm, Thickness 1 cm

*Excavated in 1976 from the tomb of Fu Hao,
Anyang, Henan Province*

163

Jade figure with protruding object

Late Shang (1300–1046 BC)

Height 7 cm, Width 3.5 cm

Excavated in 1976 from the tomb of Fu Hao, Anyang, Henan Province

This yellowish-brown jade kneeling figure, carved in the round, rests his hands on his thighs. His long, braided hair coils from ear to ear; we see traces of hair on his crown. His hat is hoop-shaped, the front curling back like a wave. This object can be hung by a hole on the crown; another small hole in front is blocked. His face is long and flat, his lower jaw raised and sharp. He has long eyebrows, large oval eyes, broad nose, firmly closed mouth and square ears. His long buttoned gown has lapels and long narrow sleeves, is pulled in at the waist with a belt and decorated with a square design. A long piece of cloth hangs over his front and he wears shoes. The sleeves and jacket have a double hooked cloud pattern and eye design. Over his right buttock are traces of a silkworm pattern, the heads resembling the auspicious Chinese 'ruyi' symbol. A broad-handled object protrudes from his back, its ends scrolling into cloud shapes, cloud designs on one side and silkworm designs on the other, resembling those on his gown. His finely decorated clothes and imposing bearing suggest he belongs to the upper ranks of society. Most distinctive is the protruding object, but the hat is also interesting, resembling a roll of silk. One of the most precious jades of the late Shang, with very fine engraving, it is a useful source for research into Shang headgear, clothing and ornament. Some scholars believe this is not a male figure but is Fu Hao herself. (Zhang Runping)

164

Jade phoenix pendant

Late Shang (1300–1046 BC)

Length 13.8 cm, Width 3.2 cm,
Thickness 0.8 cm

*Excavated in 1976 from tomb of Fu Hao, Anyang,
Henan Province*

The piece is made of yellowish-grey jade using
openwork engraving. It shows a phoenix, the
symbol of female imperial power, with its head
turned backwards, a cockerel-like crest, round
eyes, a sharp beak, protruding chest, and the
body with short wings and long double tail
feathers forming a curve. Its claws are depicted
and a small pierced protuberance on its back
was used to suspend it from a belt. The wing
feathers are depicted by lines. It has a beautiful,
fluent form and is exquisitely worked.
(Zhang Runping)

165

Jade figure in obeisance

Early Western Zhou (c.11th century BC)

Height 7.3 cm, Width 2.5 cm,
Thickness 1.3 cm

*Excavated in 1959 from a tomb
in the eastern suburbs of Luoyang,
Henan Province*

167

Jade axe handle with
phoenix design

Mid Western Zhou (c.10th century BC)

Height 7.2 cm, Width 3.8 cm,
Thickness 0.4 cm

*Excavated in Puducun, Changanxian,
Xian, Shaanxi Province*

166

Semi-circular disk with
double-headed design

Western Zhou (1046–711 BC)

Length 10 cm, Width 1.9 cm,
Thickness 0.5 cm

168

Agate beads and jade cylinder necklace

Late Western Zhou (c.8th century BC)

Total Length 54 cm; Jade cylinders:
Length 2–2.7 cm, Width 0.9–1.2 cm;
Agate beads: Diameter 0.5–0.8 cm

*Excavated in 1956–57 in tomb No.
1820 at the Guo cemetery, Sanmenxia,
Henan Province*

169

Dragon pattern jade rings

Spring and Autumn (770–476 BC)

Diameter 3.7 cm, Diameter of hole 1.2 cm,
Thickness 0.4 cm

*Excavated in 1957 from Shangcunling,
Sanmenxia, Henan Province*

170

Group of jade pendants

Early Warring States (475–376 BC)

Length of dragon piece 7.1 cm,
Diameters: large agate ring 5.5 cm,
small agate ring 3 cm, jade ring 3.6 cm

*Excavated in 1955 from tomb No. 1316 at
Zhongzhoulu, Luoyang, Henan Province*

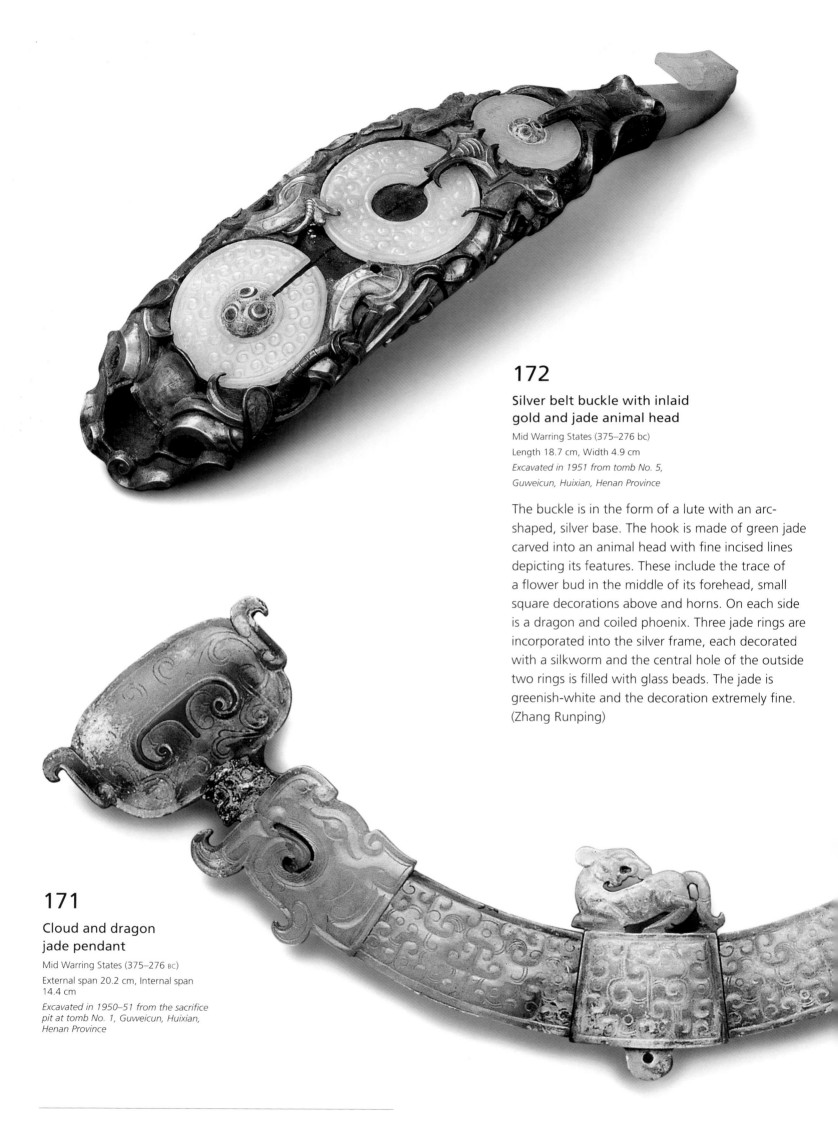

172

Silver belt buckle with inlaid gold and jade animal head

Mid Warring States (375–276 bc)
Length 18.7 cm, Width 4.9 cm
Excavated in 1951 from tomb No. 5, Guweicun, Huixian, Henan Province

The buckle is in the form of a lute with an arc-shaped, silver base. The hook is made of green jade carved into an animal head with fine incised lines depicting its features. These include the trace of a flower bud in the middle of its forehead, small square decorations above and horns. On each side is a dragon and coiled phoenix. Three jade rings are incorporated into the silver frame, each decorated with a silkworm and the central hole of the outside two rings is filled with glass beads. The jade is greenish-white and the decoration extremely fine. (Zhang Runping)

171

Cloud and dragon jade pendant

Mid Warring States (375–276 bc)

External span 20.2 cm, Internal span 14.4 cm

Excavated in 1950–51 from the sacrifice pit at tomb No. 1, Guweicun, Huixian, Henan Province

173

Openwork jade pendant of paired dragons

Mid Warring States (375–276 BC)

Length 8.9 cm, Width 3.4 cm, Thickness 0.3 cm

Excavated in 1957 from tomb No. 1, Changtaiguan, Xinyangxian, Henan Province

174

Jade phoenix pendant

Mid Warring States (375–276 BC)

Length 7.6 cm, Width 3.4 cm, Thickness 0.4 cm

Excavated in 1951 from tomb No. 2, Guweicun, Huixian, Henan Province

175

**Dragon-patterned
jade *bi* disk**

Western Han (206 BC – AD 8)
Diameter 26.3 cm

176

Jade burial suit with gold ties

Western Han (206 BC – AD 8)
Length 182 cm, Width at shoulders 49 cm
*Excavated in 1973 from the Han period tomb
No. 40 at Bajiaolangcun, Dingxian, Hebei Province*

This is made from a green jade with impurities showing
as coloured patches. The suit comprises 1,203 jade
disks tied with 2,567 gold threads. The suit can be
divided into five sections: the head, jacket, trousers,
shoes and gloves. There is a round disk of jade on the
crown of the head, and the face and nose parts have
a convex shape. Both sides of the chest use triangular
pieces, the glove sections are fist shaped and the foot
pieces are squared off across the toes. A rectangular
jade pillow was excavated along with this suit with a
concave arch made to hold the head of the suit. There
were also five pieces of jade placed in the orifices of the
deceased.

    Jade burial suits can be traced back to the Eastern
Zhou period and were used to preserve the body of
deceased rulers. (Zhang Runping)

177

Jade bowl with gold rim

Sui (581–618)
Height 4.1 cm, Diameter at mouth 5.6 cm,
Diameter at foot 2.9 cm
*Excavated in 1957 from Li Jingxun's tomb,
Xian, Shaanxi Province*

178

Jade lion

Tang (618–907)

Height 5 cm, Length 7.8 cm, Width 3.2 cm

179

Jade comb back decorated with crab apples

Tang (618–907)

Length 10.5 cm, Width 4.4 cm, Thickness 0.2 cm

Excavated in the 1950s from a Tang tomb in Xian, Shaanxi Province

180

Jade lotus petal hat

Song (960–1279)

Height 7.4 cm, Length 10.6 cm, Width 7.4 cm

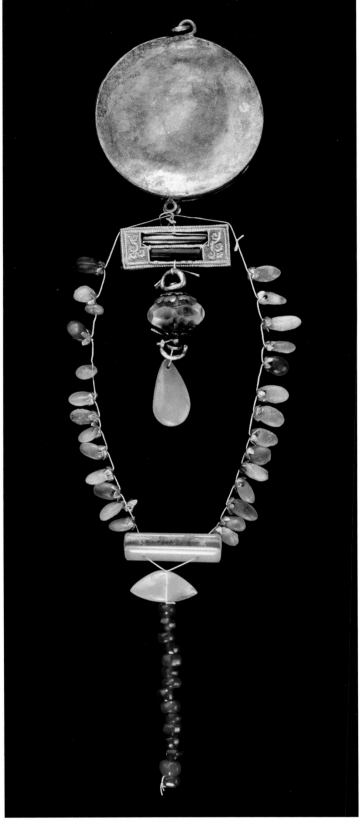

181

Double-figure jade
knife handle

Jin (1115–1234)

Height 9.5 cm,
Diameter at base 2.4 cm

182

Waist pendant of gold and silver gilt
case, crystal, agate and jade beads

Jin (1115–1234)

Overall Length 37.7 cm, Diameter of silver box 8.4 cm,
Length of rectangular gold decoration 5.9 cm

*Excavated in 1973 from a Jin tomb at Zhongxing,
Suibinxian, Heilongjiang Province*

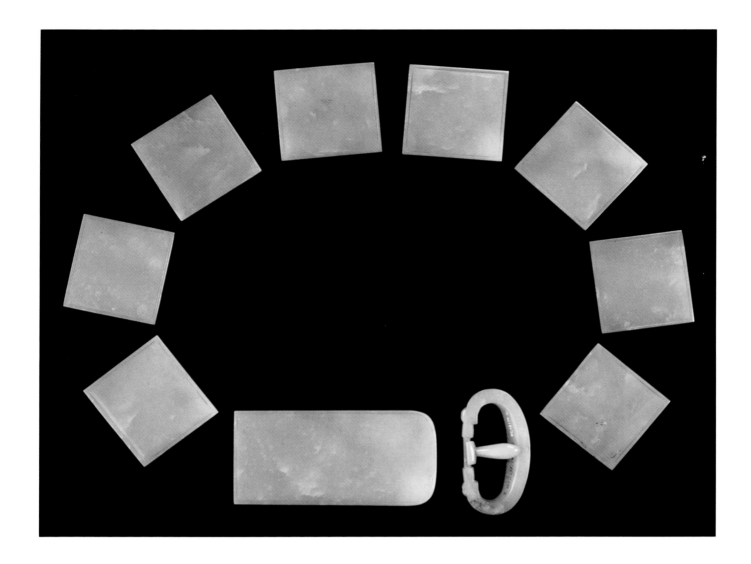

183

Jade belt plaques

Yuan (1271–1368)

Length 84 cm, Buckle: Length 7 cm, Width 6.9 cm, Thickness 0.8 cm; End plaque: Length 14.5 cm, Width 7 cm, Thickness 0.8 cm

Excavated in 1955 from Fan Wenhu's tomb, Anqing, Anhui Province

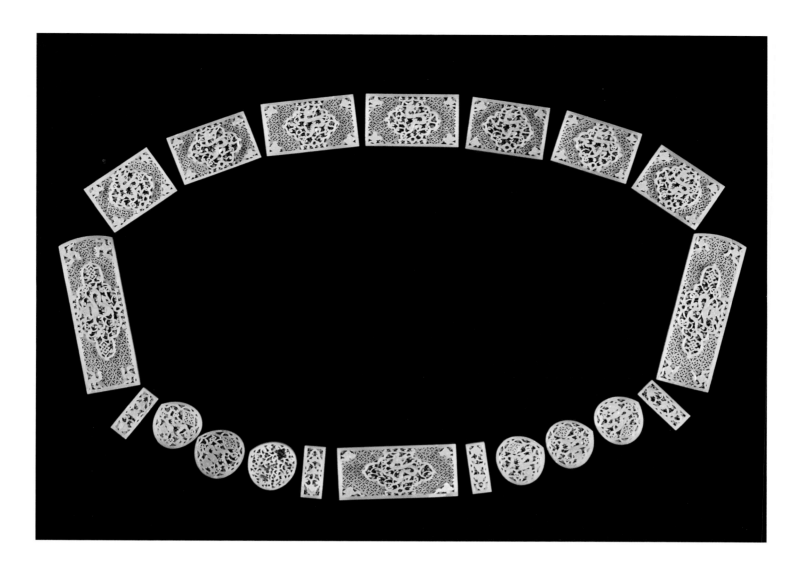

184

Jade belt plaques with openwork dragon design

Jiajing reign period (1522–1566), Ming

End plaques: Length 13 cm, Width 4.4 cm;
Rectangular plaques: Length 6–9.8 cm,
Width 4.1–4.4 cm; Small strip-shaped plaques:
Length 4.3 cm, Width 1.7 cm; Peach-shaped plaques:
Length 4 cm, Width 4 cm

*Excavated in 1958 from Zhu Houye's tomb,
Nanchengxian, Jiangxi Province*

This set of 20 openwork pieces of white jade forms a belt and comprises two rectangular end pieces, eight rectangular plaques, four small strip-shaped plaques and six peach-shaped plaques. The end and the long plaques have a design of dragons and clouds set among a base design of coins, the Buddhist swastika character and flowers and plants. The peach-shaped plaques have an openwork dragon and the small strips, one of clouds. The dragons are all in profile, with a rolled cloud-shaped raised nose, open mouths and long beards floating behind them. Their slim bodies are completely adorned with scales and their long legs incised with fine lines to suggest hair, ending in four claws with ball-shaped pads. Their tails bifurcate and transform into clouds. The technique of the decoration shows that it was made in the Jia jing period.

Leather belts adorned with jade plaques like this were used by Ming officials when in their official robes to indicate their rank and role. (Zhang Runping)

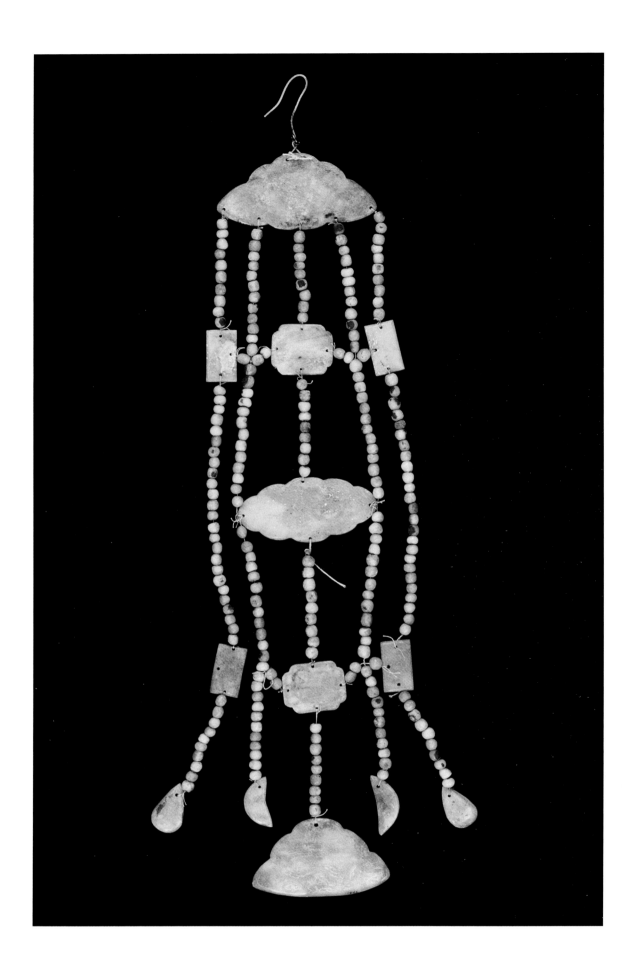

185

Jade pendant plaques with cloud and dragon designs outlined in gold

Wanli reign period (1573–1620), Ming

Length 50.5 cm

Excavated in 1957 from Shisanling, Changpingxian, Beijing

186

Jade vessel with animal face design and animal handles

Ming (1368–1644)

Height 17.5 cm, Diameter at mouth 13.3 cm,
Diameter at base 9.4 cm

187

Double-phoenix-handle jade bowl

Ming (1368–1644)

Height 7 cm, Diameter at mouth 8.6 cm,
Diameter at foot 4 cm, Thickness 0.4 cm

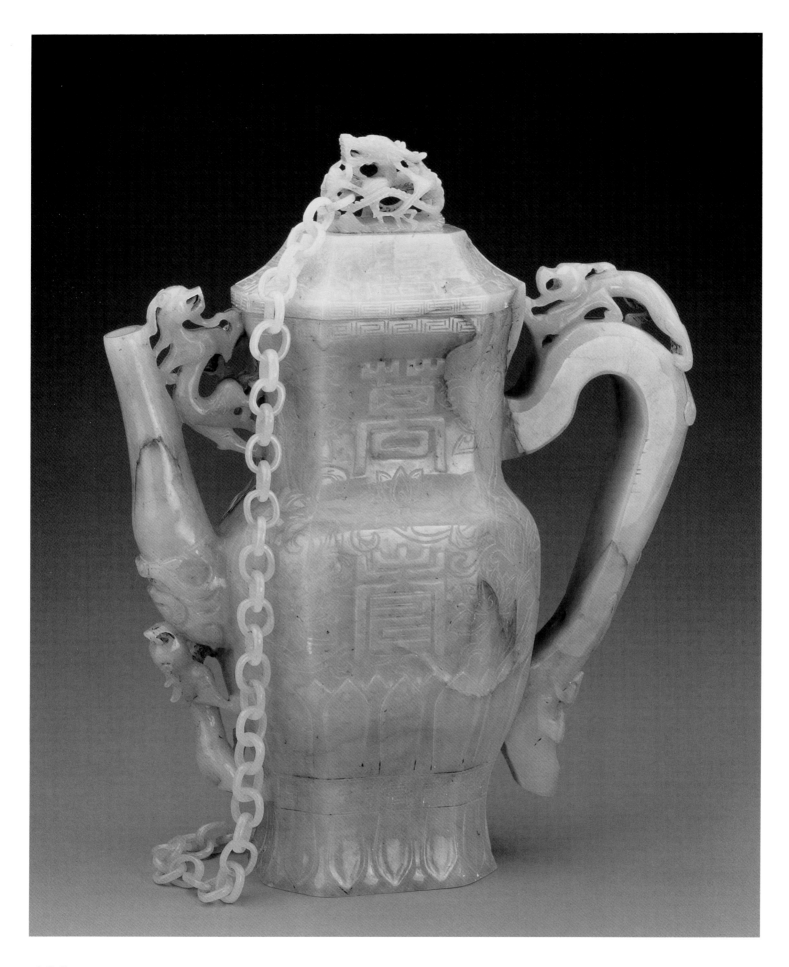

188

**Jade pot with longevity
and good fortune design**

Ming (1368–1644)

Height 36.5 cm, Mouth 13.4 x 10 cm,
Base 11.5 x 8 cm

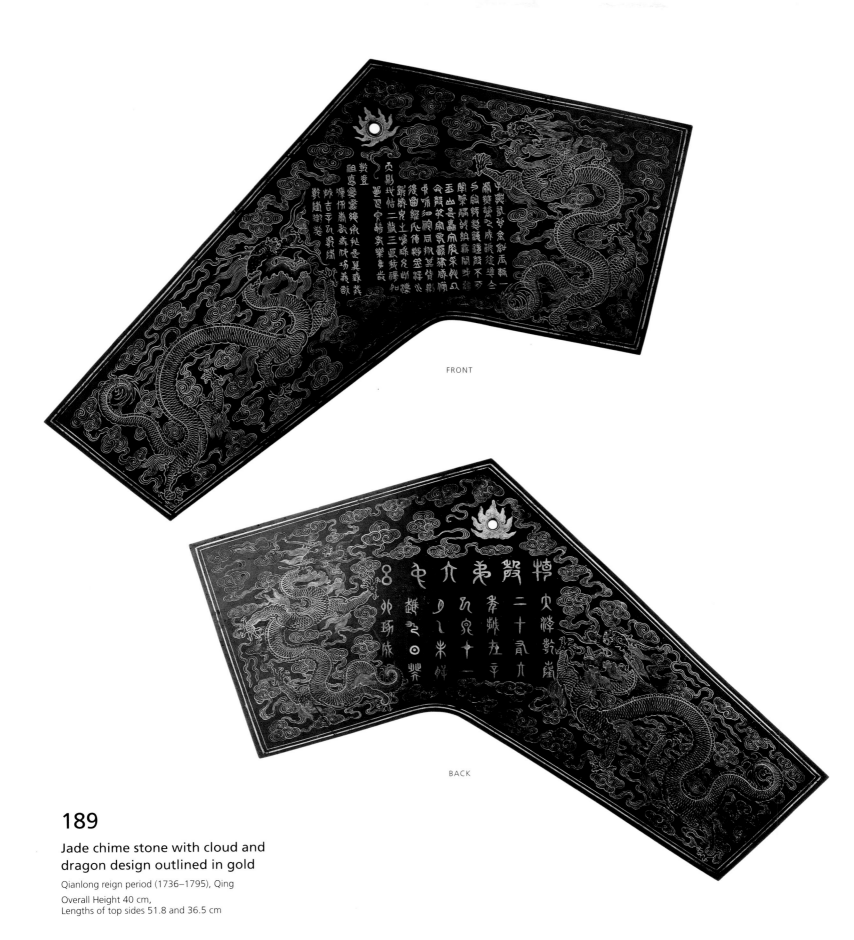

FRONT

BACK

189

Jade chime stone with cloud and dragon design outlined in gold

Qianlong reign period (1736–1795), Qing
Overall Height 40 cm,
Lengths of top sides 51.8 and 36.5 cm

Made of dark green jade the chime stone is shaped like a set square. Both sides, both sections and the edges are covered with a design of dragons playing with a pearl and clouds outlined in gold. The central section of the front has characters of seal script inlaid with gold. A hole piercing the jade is decorated with a fiery pearl design and in the central part there is an inscription in gold.

The chime stone is an ancient musical instrument made from stone or jade. This is a chime used by the Qing emperor in imperial sacrificial rituals and important events to reproduce classical music of the Qin period and that of Shao and Yue, as mentioned by Confucius. This used sets of 12 different-sized chime stones, suspended from a frame and struck to make a sound, each with a different note. Use of jade from the town of Khotan, the primary supplier for China, was strictly regulated and this is a piece of pure jade, which has been beautifully and precisely fashioned and decorated with exquisite carving. It is a treasure of Qing imperial jades. (Zhang Runping)

190

Jade bottle with plum blossom design

Qing (1644–1911)

Height 28 cm,
Diameter of mouth 7.5 cm

191

Double-linked bowls with six dragonfly handles with rings

Qing (1644–1911)

Height 6.7 cm, greatest Length 23.5 cm;
greatest Width 15.6 cm

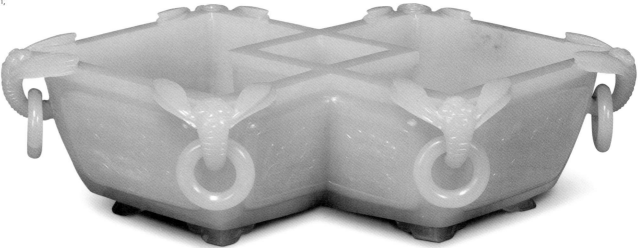

192

Jade teapot

Qing (1644–1911)

Height 14.7 cm,
Diameter at mouth 7.6 cm,
Diameter at base 6.7 cm

193

Jade gourd-shaped
water container

Qing (1644–1911)

Height 8 cm, Length 18.6 cm,
Width 12 cm

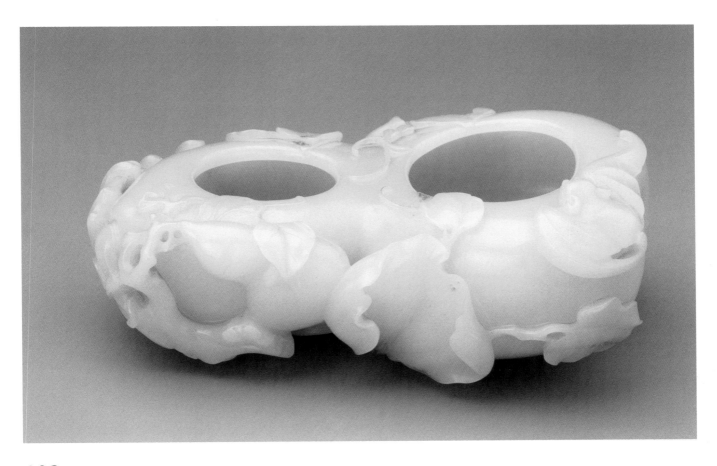

GOLD AND SILVER

The production of gold and silver wares forms an important chapter in the history of Chinese arts and crafts, as well as being a repository for the aesthetics of the ancient cultures of China. The Museum collection contains objects from each of the important periods from the Shang to the Qing, comprehensively reflecting the development of gold and silver technology in China.

It is evident from archaeological artefacts that gold and silver objects appeared as early as the Shang period, for example, the decorative gold earrings excavated from the Baiyan site at Taiguxian, Shanxi Province and the Shang tombs at Liujiahe in Beijing. Gold pieces from this period were generally small and delicate with simple forms, little or no decoration and regional characteristics. The flourishing of cast bronze technology in the Shang advanced the development of gold and silver production.

In the Spring and Autumn and Warring States periods, the production areas of gold and silver expanded greatly and the number of types increased. Typical of the Central Plains are those excavated from the Wei tombs at Guweicun, Huixian, Henan Province and King Zhongshan's tomb at Pingshanxian, Hebei Province. The most beautiful objects of the southern regions are those from Zeng Houyi's tomb at Suixian, Hubei Province. The objects of the peoples of the northern grasslands are very different in style and have distinctive features, such as the large hoard discovered from the Xiongnu tombs at Aluchaideng, Inner Mongolia, with vivid relief decorations of animals, reflecting the life of the grasslands.

The Han sees the appearance of inlaid wares, greater in number than in previous periods. There were significant advances in the manufacturing processes at this time, with gold and silver inlaid into bronze and iron, but also the use of gold leaf and gold paste to decorate lacquers and silk textiles. Apart from decorative wares, gold and silver were used in the Han for making horse tackle and chariot parts, belt buckles, seals and medical needles. In the succeeding Wei, Jin and Northern and Southern dynasties period we see a trend towards an amalgamation of the different regional styles and of the distinctive traits of the northern peoples. At the same time, gold and silver technology gradually matured and expanded in scope. The Sui and Tang was the peak of gold and silver manufacture.

The gold necklace with embedded gems and the head ornament from Li Jingxun's tomb in the western suburbs of Xian are superlative pieces of Sui-period manufacture. The Tang made use of more complex processes such as engraved designs, openwork, welding and polishing. The use of gold and silver objects also increased. Decorative pieces continued to be made, but gold and silver was also used for eating utensils, vessels, medical equipment, and objects for everyday and religious use. At the same time there was outside influence, so that Tang wares show features from many different peoples in both their form and technique.

In the Song period gold and silver became much more widely used, inheriting and developing the emerging secularization, the trend towards the commodification of goods, and all the technical manufacturing skills. Based on this, the gold and silver industry continued to prosper in the Ming period. The most important items from the Ming in the Museum's collection are a crown and face cover, excavated from the Ming imperial tomb of Zhu Houye, Nanchengxian, Jiangxi Province and from the Dingling imperial mausoleum near Beijing, representing the best of Ming-period pieces. The Qing continued to develop the Ming tradition of fine workmanship to a state of extreme refinement, seen especially in pieces handed down by the court, and the techniques reached new heights, such as inlaying with precious stones, engraving and the use of cut and drops of jade. (Wang Zhan)

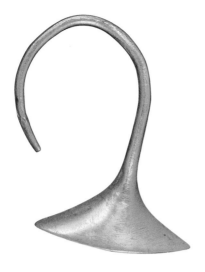

194

Gold earring

Shang (1600–1046 BC)

Length 3.5 cm, Width 2 cm,
Weight 6.7 g

*Excavated in 1977 from Shang
tomb at Liujiahe, Pingguxian, Beijing*

195

Gold earrings

Shang (1600–1046 BC)

Length 4.6 cm, Width 3.8 cm,
Weight 4.5 g, 5.62 g

*Excavated in 1980 from Baiyan
site, Taiguxian, Shanxi Province*

196

Gold plaque showing four tigers
eating an ox

Warring States (475–221 BC)

Length 12.7 cm, Width 7.4 cm, Weight 237.625 g

*Excavated in 1972 from Aluchaideng, Hanggin Banner,
Inner Mongolia*

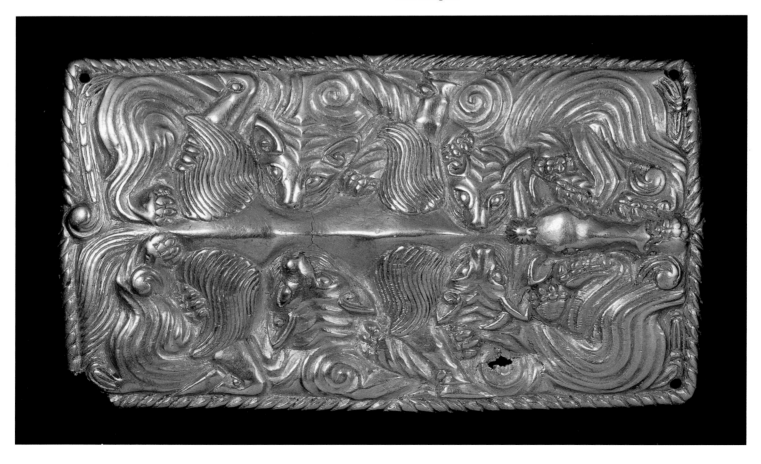

197

Gold plaque with inlaid turquoise and animal design

Warring States (475–221 BC)

Length 4.6 cm, Width 3 cm, Weight 22.25 g

Excavated in 1972 from Aluchaideng, Hanggin Banner, Inner Mongolia

198

Copper spear end with inlaid gold

Western Han (206 BC – AD 8)

Length 15.8 cm, Diameter 2.1 cm

Excavated in 1968 from a Han tomb at Manchengxian, Hebei Province

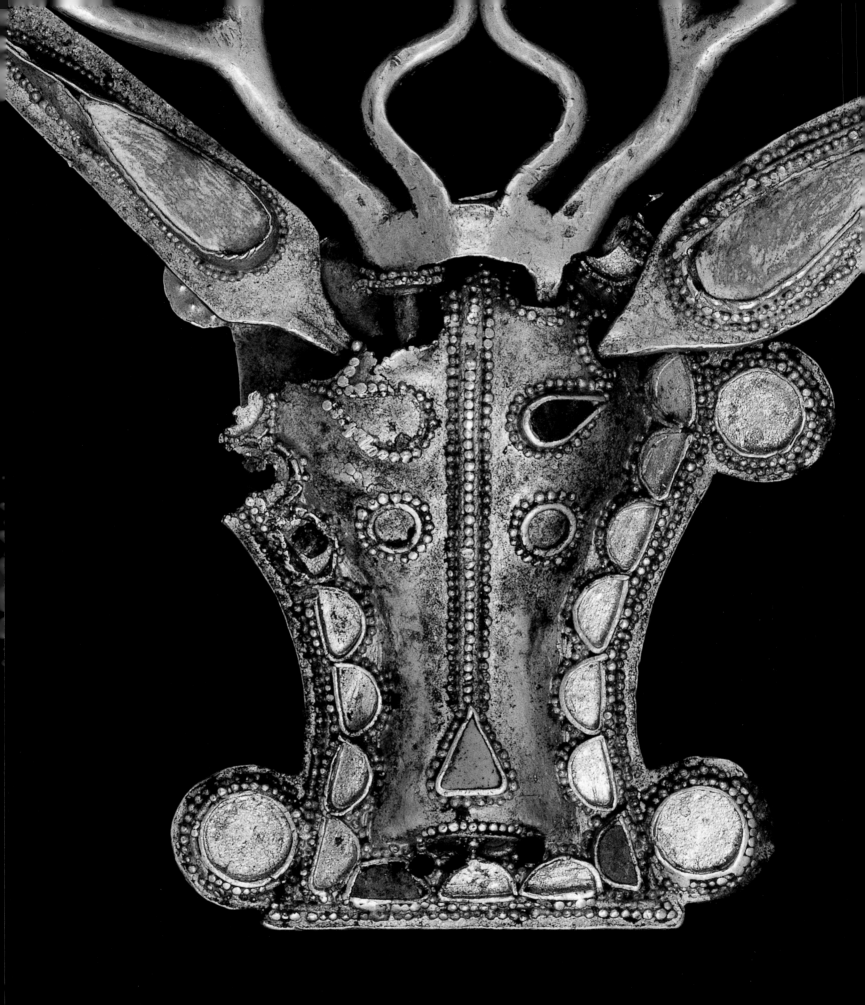

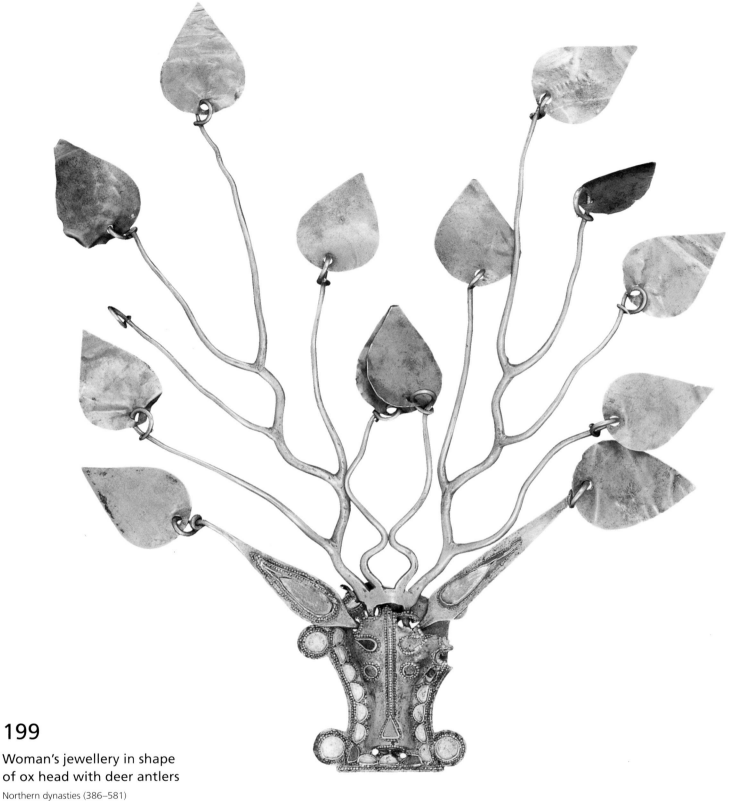

199

**Woman's jewellery in shape
of ox head with deer antlers**

Northern dynasties (386–581)
Length 19.4 cm, Weight 87.37 g
Excavated in 1981 from Dardan
Muming'an United Banner, Inner Mongolia

The cast ox head and antlers are very attractive with their distinct and lifelike modelling. The ox face has a broad forehead, which then curves inward at the cheeks and outward again at the horns and mouth, flattening at the end. The contours of the different parts of the face are edged with a fish egg design, inlaid with white, blue and green stones. His horns are in the form of deer antlers with the two main branches splitting into four or five sections, the tip of each bent into a small ring. Attached to these like leaves are moveable peach-shaped disks; 13 remain of the original 14.

During the Wei, Jin and Northern and Southern dynasties period, the use of such ornaments was popular among the peoples who lived in the north. When worn by the Xianbei women at this time the antlers swayed as they walked causing the gold leaves to tremble: this was a habit that can be traced back to the Han period. Not only was this piece very fashionable but it was also a symbol of the rank of the wearer. (Yu Lu)

200

Head ornament of gold, silver and pearls in flower design

Sui (581–618)

Length of silver support 6 cm, Width 3.2 cm

Excavated in 1957 from Li Jingxun's tomb, Western Xian, Shaanxi Province

201

Inlaid gold and silver
incense burner

Tang (618–907)

Diameter 4.8 cm

*Excavated in 1963 from an underground
storehouse at Shapocun in the south-
east of Xian, Shaanxi Province*

FRONT

BACK

This spherical incense burner is suspended from a chain
attached to a small loop on its top. The openwork design is
of flowers and there is also an engraved design of flowers
and birds. The top and bottom hemispheres are separate and
are joined by a hinge. Inside the lower hemisphere are two
concentric hemispherical bowls, the outer one attached to the
body, and the inner one attached in such a way that, regardless
of how much the ball is rotated to distribute the incense smoke,
the small bowl always stays level, and the incense and ash
remain inside.

This piece is exquisitely designed to be used either as a
personal adornment or in a room. Incense burners were also
part of Buddhist ceremonies and Buddhist scriptural scrolls were
often stored with spice bags with the intention of warding off
evil. (Wang Zhan)

202

Silver wine cup with a flower and bird lotus petal design and a stem foot

Tang (618–907)

Height 5 cm, Diameter of mouth 7.2 cm, Diameter at base 3.8 cm

Excavated in 1963 from an underground storehouse at Shapocun in the south-east of Xian, Shaanxi Province

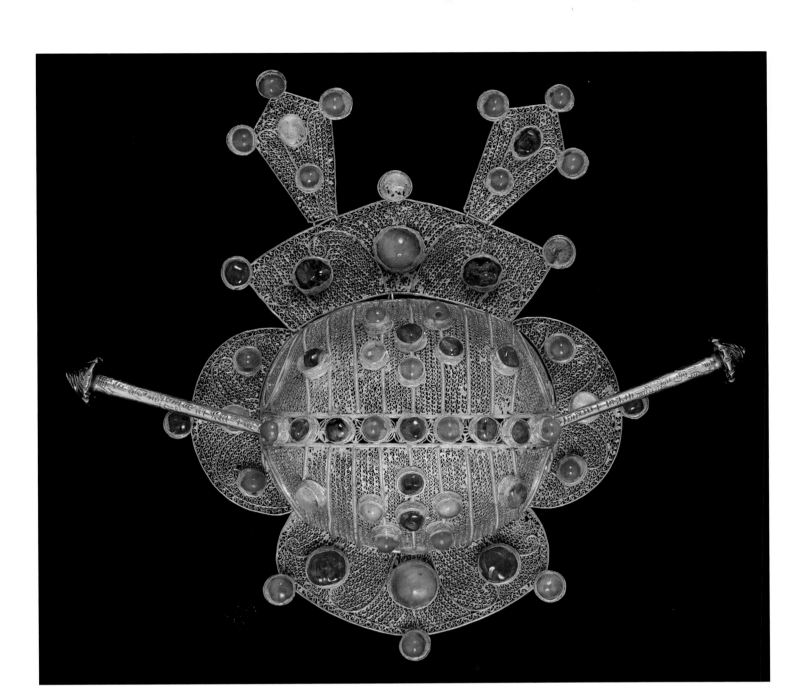

This headaddress is in the shape of an upturned oval alms bowl, made of four filigree sections: crown, peak, brim and tongue. The crown rests on an oval gold band and has two arch-shaped strips running horizontally across it, each inlaid with nine precious stones, and nine evenly distributed strips running the other way to support the hat on the head. There is a peak and brims on the back and sides, the back one joining to two tongues, all inlaid with precious stones. A small hole on each side of the bottom edge of the two horizontal strips holds a gold hairpin; there is another hairpin hole in the middle of the front part of the crown. The hairpin heads are umbrella-shaped and engraved with decorative designs; their shafts are incised with characters reading 'Made of five taels worth of gold in the tenth lunar month of the 26th year of the Jia jing reign period [1547]'. This piece is peerless, its 55 symmetrically inlaid gems enhancing each other's beauty, its exquisitely fashioned thin gold thread like hair. This rare treasure displays the superlative skills of Ming dynasty gold and silver technology. (Wan Zhan)

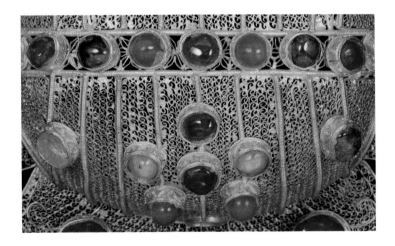

203

Gold headdress inlaid with precious stones and with hairpins

Jiajing reign period, 26th year (1547), Ming
Length 11 cm
Excavated in 1958 from the Ming imperial tomb of Houye, Nanchengxian, Jiangxi Province

4

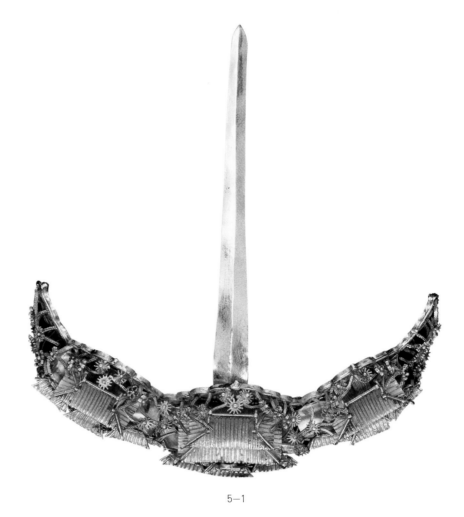

5—1

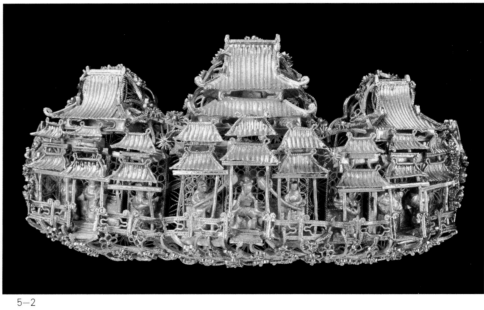

5—2

6

7

8

9

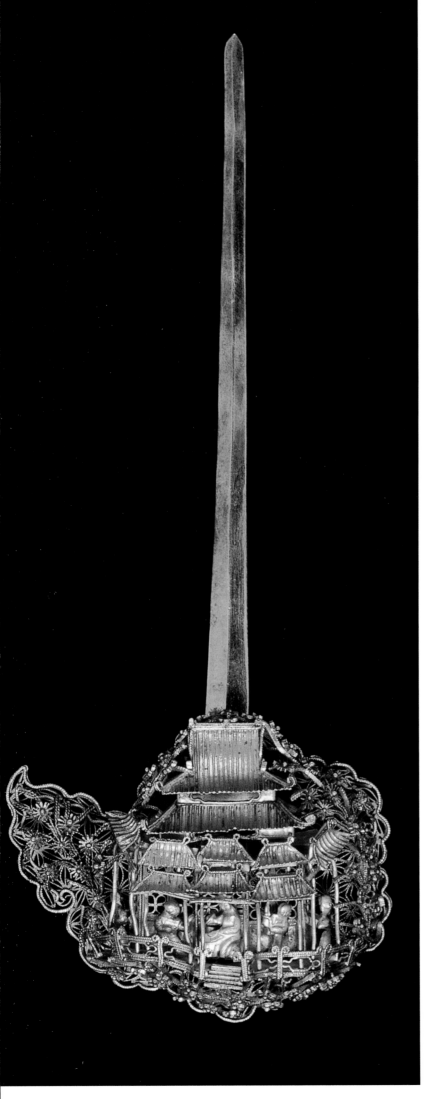

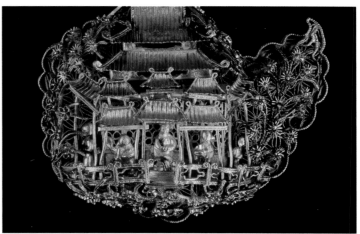

2

3

204

Gold hairpins with design of figures on a pavilion

Ming (1368–1644)

Overall Height 5.1–20 cm,
Width 3.3–9.8 cm, Weight 43.4–118.9 g

Filigree hairpin head (left): Height 17.9 cm,
Width 6.7 cm, Weight 58 g

*Excavated in 1958 from the Ming imperial
tomb of Zhu Houye, Nanchengxian,
Jiangxi Province*

The Museum collection contains nine similar gold hairpins
from the same tomb, all showing figures in a pavilion
and used by Zhu Houye's consort. In their design and
manufacture they show the very best of the goldworkers'
skills and are superlative examples of filigree work, using
extremely fine gold threads, woven to form a complex and
dazzling design yet remaining light enough to be useable.
In the hands of a master craftsman this everyday object is
transformed into a refined work of art. The filigree hairpin
head (to the left) consists of a two-sided pavilion, its edges
embellished with flowing clouds. Inside this are five figures,
including the mistress sitting in the middle, with a female
attendant on each side. The base is a flat rhomboid shape
with pointed bottom. This is one of two symmetrical
hairpins to be used on either side of the head. (Wang Zhan)

206

Gold bracelet inlaid with precious stones

Ming (1368–1644)

Diameter 6.5 cm, Width 2.6 cm, Weight 139 g

Excavated in 1958 from the Ming imperial tomb of Houye, Nanchengxian, Jiangxi Province

205

Gold pendant with phoenix design

Jiajing reign period 26th year (1547), Ming

Height 16.5 cm, Width 7.5 cm, Weight 71.8 g

Excavated in 1958 from the Ming imperial tomb of Houye, Nanchengxian, Jiangxi Province

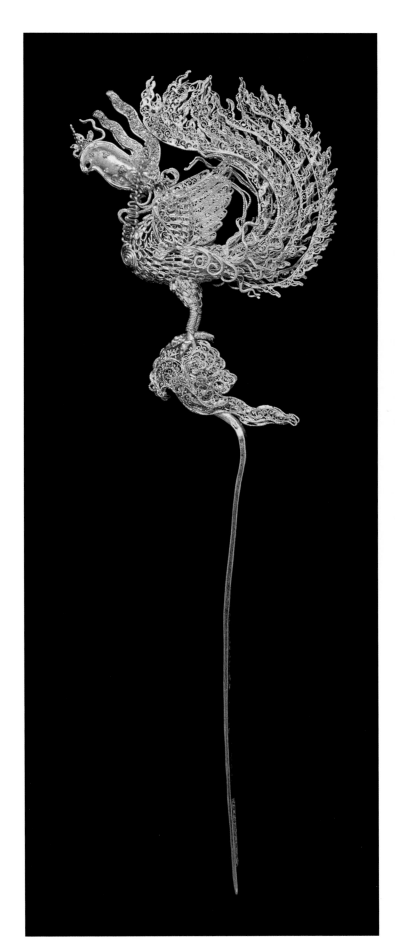

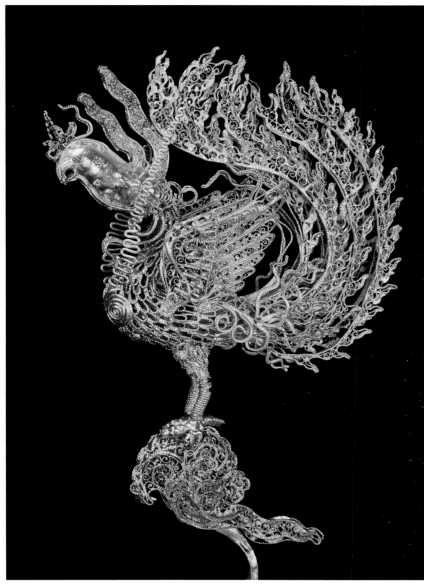

207

Gold hairpin in the form of a phoenix

Yongle reign period 22nd year (1424), Ming

Length 22.3 cm, Weight 75.7 g

Excavated in 1958 from the Ming imperial tomb of Houye, Nanchengxian, Jiangxi Province

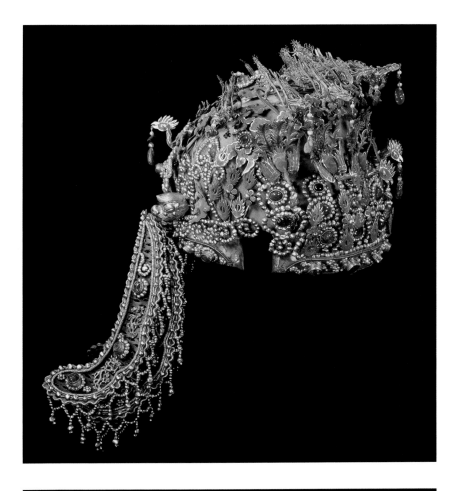

208

Headdress with design of nine dragons and nine phoenix with pearls, precious stones and green jade among gold

Ming (1368–1644)

Overall Height 48.5 cm, Height of crown 27 cm, Diameter 23.7 cm, Weight 2320 g

Excavated in 1958 from Dingling imperial mausoleum, Changping, Beijing

This piece is the phoenix headdress of Emperor Shenzong's imperial concubine, Xiao Jing, and is made on a skeleton of lacquered bamboo covered with silk fabric. The crown is encircled by nine large golden dragons prancing among the clouds holding drops in their mouths made from two small pearls and two gemstones, and there is a row of eight gemstones inlaid into the bottom of the dragons' feet. Eight gold phoenix match the dragons, also with pearl drops in their mouths, their lower parts embedded with four lines of gemstones. There are three rows of inlaid gems in the crown of the hat and one row extending to the front, with the top two rows containing eight stones and the lower two rows having seven. Each setting is encircled with a design made of pearls. In the centre of the rear section there is another gold phoenix holding a pearl drop in its mouth, each side inlaid with one stone and with a row of five inlaid stones below. Three moving fan sections hang from each side of the rim, each decorated with two dragons with inlaid pearls and spots of jade and three gems. There are five gems along the back and seven on the crown.

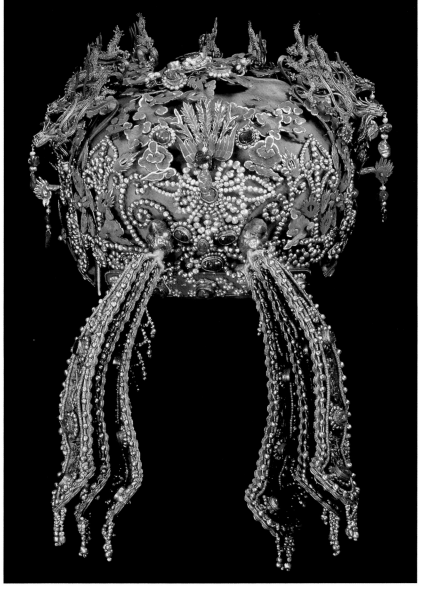

This crown contains over 1,000 inlaid gemstones and more than 5,000 pearls. Four phoenix crowns were found in the Dingling imperial mausoleum: the first with three dragons and two phoenix; the second with nine dragons and nine phoenix; the third with twelve dragons and nine phoenix; and the last with six dragons and three phoenix. The dragon and phoenix are symbols of the emperor and empress, respectively. The filigree work gives the dragons a three-dimensional feel and the use of pearls to decorate the inlaid gemstones and outline the designs creates a dazzling effect. The phoenix crowns all use green for the base, red for the sides, and blue for the flowing clouds, the dragon and phoenix. They are splendid and majestic pieces. (Wang Zhan)

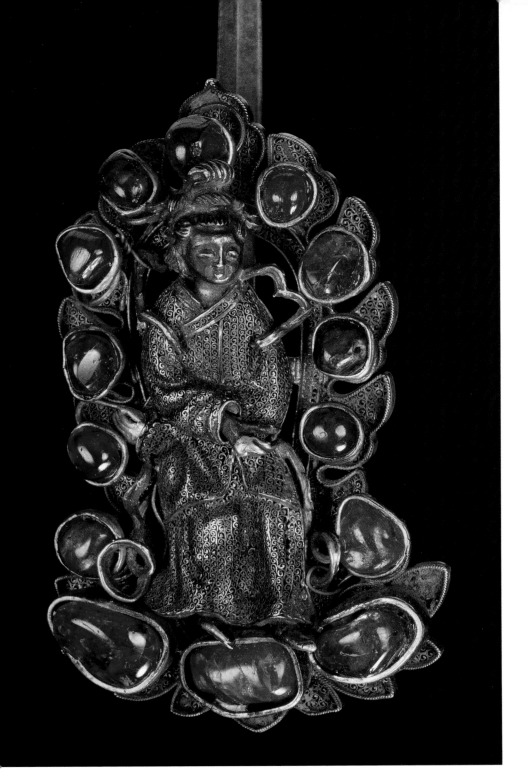

209

Gilt silver hairpin with inlaid gems
and a figure of an immortal

Ming (1368–1644)

Length 14 cm

*Excavated in 1958 in the Dingling imperial mausoleum,
Changping, Beijing*

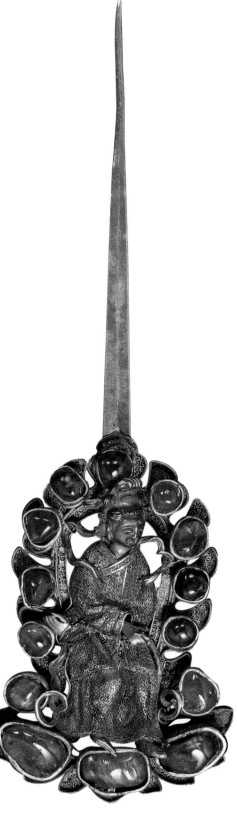

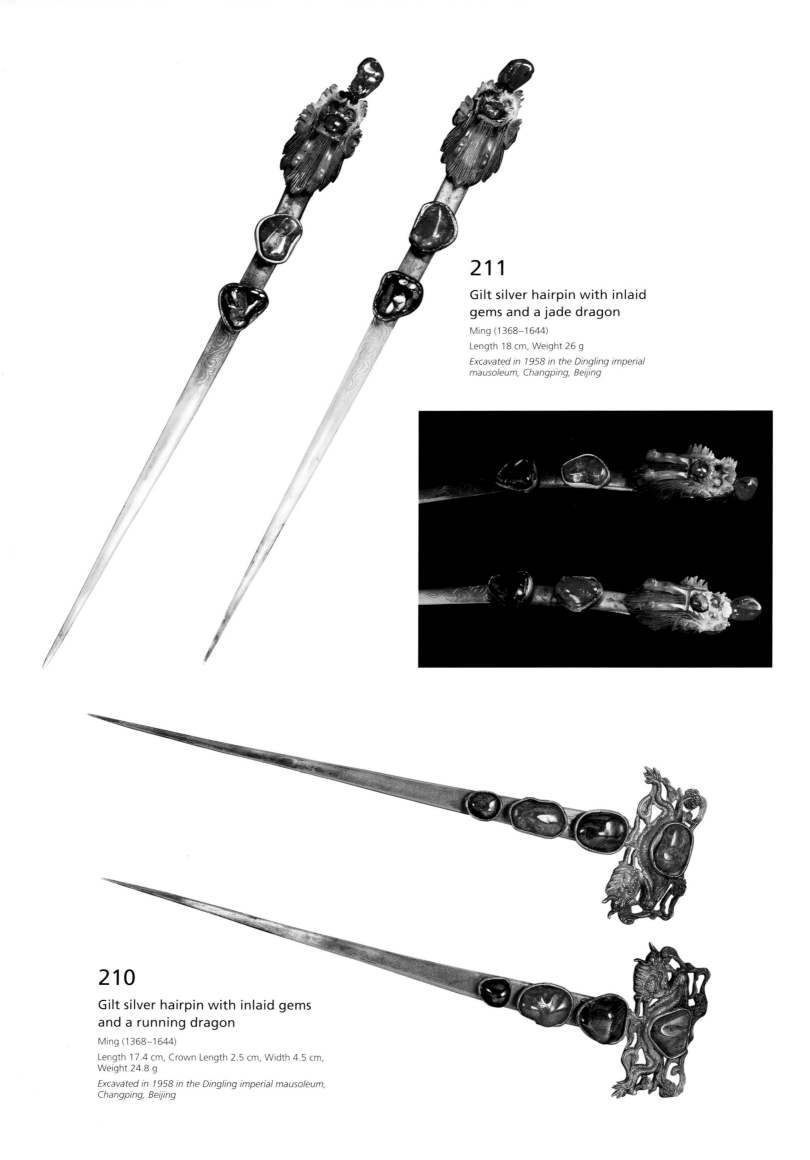

211

Gilt silver hairpin with inlaid gems and a jade dragon

Ming (1368–1644)

Length 18 cm, Weight 26 g

Excavated in 1958 in the Dingling imperial mausoleum, Changping, Beijing

210

Gilt silver hairpin with inlaid gems and a running dragon

Ming (1368–1644)

Length 17.4 cm, Crown Length 2.5 cm, Width 4.5 cm, Weight 24.8 g

Excavated in 1958 in the Dingling imperial mausoleum, Changping, Beijing

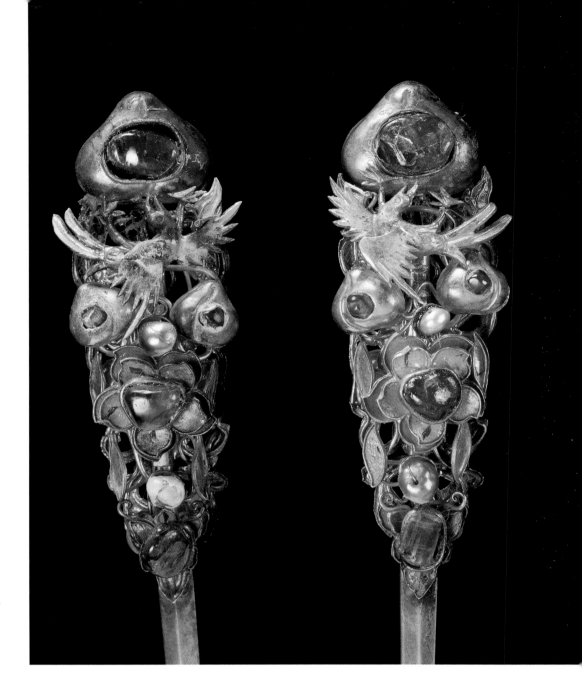

212

Gilt silver hairpin with inlaid stones and a phoenix and peach

Ming (1368–1644)

Excavated in 1958 in the Dingling imperial mausoleum, Changping, Beijing

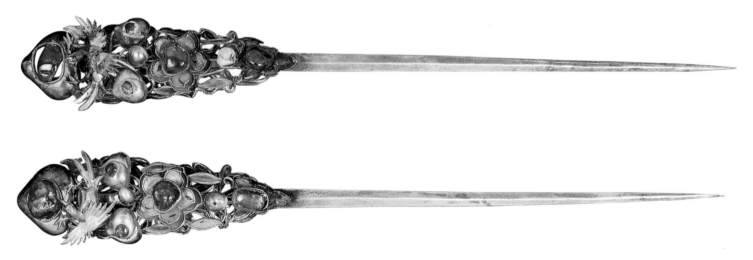

214

Pair of gold bracelets

Ming (1368–1644)
Diameter 7.5 cm, Weight 40.84 and 40.06 g
Excavated in 1958 in the Dingling imperial mausoleum, Changping, Beijing

213

Gold ewer with dragon and phoenix design

Ming (1368–1644)

Ewer: Height 12.5 cm, Diameter at mouth 4.2 cm, Diameter of foot 5.7 cm; Cover: Height 3.1 cm, Diameter of mouth 4.5 cm; Weight 192.5 g

Excavated in 1958 in the Dingling imperial mausoleum, Changping, Beijing

215

Gold pot

Ming (1368–1644)

Height 26.5 cm, Diameter at belly 16 cm,
Diameter at mouth 9.1 cm, Diameter at base 13.9

*Excavated in 1958 in the Dingling imperial mausoleum,
Changping, Beijing*

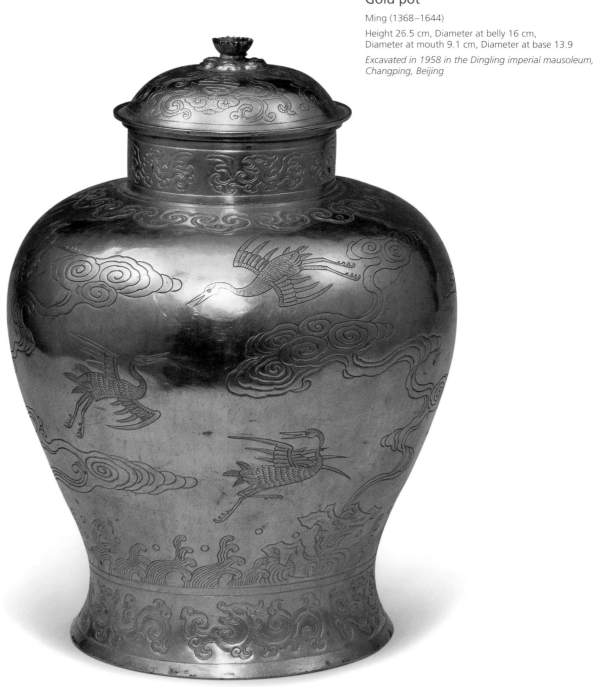

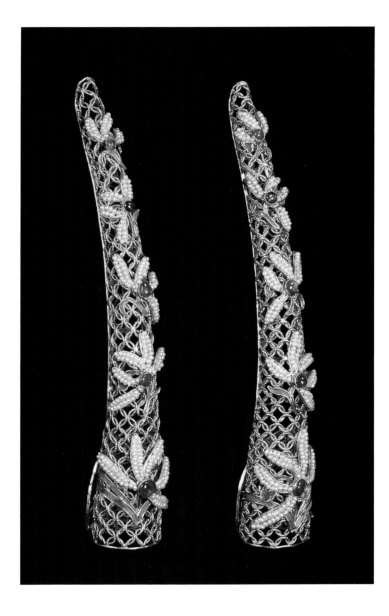

216

Gold fingernail sheaths with
inlaid stones and pearls

Qing (1644–1911)

Length 10 cm

217

Hairpin with silver shaft
and gilt kingfisher head

Qing (1644–1911)

Length 23.5 cm

218

Silver gilt neck ring with inlaid pearls

Qing (1644–1911)

Diameter 16.3 cm

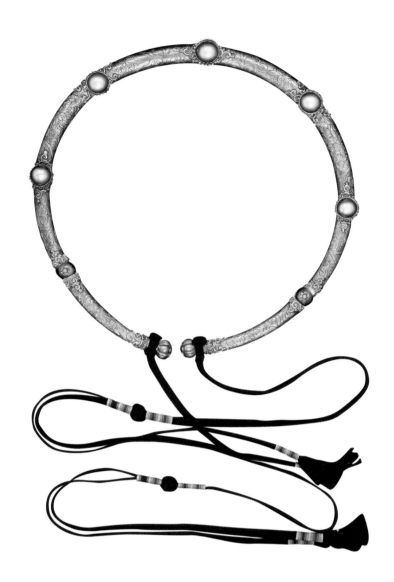

219

Silver helmet with dragon design and inlaid coral and pearls

Qing (1644–1911)

Height 12.5 cm, Diameter 21 cm

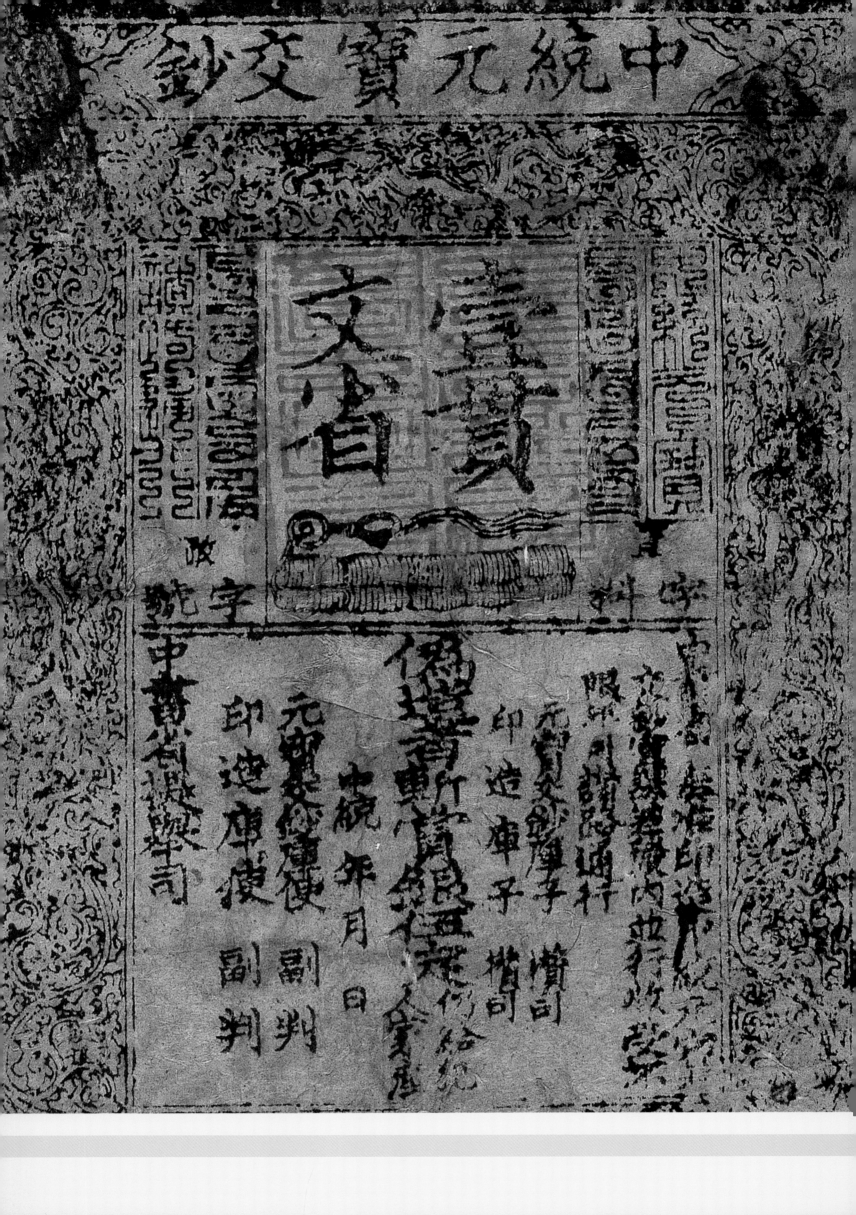

中統元寶交鈔

貳佰文

尚書省

CURRENCY

The origins of money in China date back to the Shang period, giving it a long and unbroken history and making it an example of the independent development of eastern culture. The history of Chinese money plays an important role in the world history of money, ranking alongside the great Western traditions of Rome and Greece.

Shells were used as the earliest currency in China while metal coins came into use in the 9th–8th centuries BC. The imperial decrees covering the standardization of writing, weights and measures issued by the First Emperor in the Qin dynasty was a major step in the standardization of Chinese money, with the round coin with a square hole, such as the *banliang* ('half *liang*', *liang* being a measure of weight), used to promote the unification of the country. For two thousand years, from this time to the end of the imperial period, this continued as the traditional form of coinage in China. China's currency system was also influential on the development of those of Japan, Korea, Vietnam and other neighbouring countries.

Paper money was first seen in China in the Northern Song period in the area of present-day Sichuan and was known as *jiaozi*. It was brought under government control in 1023 under the Song emperor Renzong. *Jiaozi* is the earliest paper money in the true sense; thereafter each currency was different owing to the different economic factors of each succeeding dynasty.

From the Tang, silver also became part of the monetary system and was more commonly used through the Song, Jin and Yuan until 1436 when, under the Ming emperor Yingzong, it replaced paper money as the legal tender.

The Museum's collection comprises nearly 200,000 items, including items from each period of history and each culture. This is a collection rich in content, complete in types and of great variety. It contains money from its earliest history in China through to the establishment of the People's Republic. Included are all forms of currency used in the pre-Qin period, such as cowry shells, spade-shaped and knife-shaped coins, round coins and the gold blocks and imitation cowries of the Chu state in the south-west.

From the Qin and Han periods, it includes *banliang* coins from different periods, *wuzhu* (five *zhu*, a measurement of weight) coins and examples of the more than 20 types of imperial coins issued following the currency reform of the emperor Wang Mang (r. 7–23). In the Three Kingdoms, Jin and Northern and Southern dynasties periods each state had a different type of *wuzhu* coin, dynastic money, reign period money and lucky money; *wuzhu* and *wujin* of the early and later Sui; and all kinds of *baowen* coins for each dynasty and reign period starting from the 7th century and the *Kaiyuan Tongbao* of the Tang dynasty through to the Qing, in which coins were no longer inscribed with their weight. The collection also holds gold cakes, horse hoof gold, gold *wuzhu* and silver taels of the Qin and Han periods and Northern Wei *Tianxing qinian* (7th year of Tianxing reign period) and its successor gold and silver coinage. From the Tang and Song we see gold and silver ingots. There is paper money from the Yuan, Ming and Qing periods. The collection holds a large number of precious and rare varieties of money, such as the *Si jian dang jin* spade coins of the Warring States, the long knife coins of the Qi state, *Guobao jingui zhiwan* from Wang Mang's reign, the gold-plated coin minted in 911 to commemorate the promotion of a carpenter to Supreme Commander of Tiance (*Tiance fubao*), *Jinkang tongbao* from the Song emperor Qinzong (r. 1126–27), and *Dade tongbao* coins from the Tangut empire. The *Songzi* three-holed spade coin from the Warring States found by archaeologists is also the only piece of its kind.

Apart from money itself, the Museum also has rich collections of coin moulds and printing blocks, offering further evidence for the development of Chinese currency. The printing block of the Southern Song is especially precious.

The collection also includes modern machine-made money, bank notes, pawn tickets, and presses from different periods, as well as coins and currency from different countries of the world from different periods. (Wang Liyan)

220

Primitive spade coin

Late Western Zhou (c.9th century to 771 BC)

Height 15.5 cm, Length 12 cm,
Width of foot 8.6 cm,
Width at broken shoulder 7.6 cm

221

Copper *xing* character imitation cowry shell

Warring States, Chu state (475–221 BC)
Length 2 cm, Width 1.3 cm, Weight 4 g

222

Linked spade coin with inscription *Si qian dang jin*

Warring States, Chu state (475–221 BC)
Length 8 cm, Weight 8 g

224

Three-hole spade coin with inscription *Wen yan xiang*

Late Warring States (275–221 BC)

Length 7 cm, Diameter at foot 4 cm, Weight 15.5 g

223

Knife coin with inscription *Qi zao bang chang da dao*

Warring States, Qi state (475–221 BC)

Length 18.5 cm, Width 2.9 cm, Weight 45 g

225

Round coin with inscription *Yi liu dao*

Warring States, Qi state (475–221 BC)

Diameter 3.5 cm, Weight 11 g

Handed down

226

Stamp for marking weight and measure of Ying, Chu state

Warring States, Chu state
(475–221 BC)

Length 1.7 cm, Width 1.7 cm

Excavated in from Shouxian, Anhui Province

227

Stone mould for *Qi da dao* coin

Warring States, Qi state
(475–221 BC)

Length 27 cm, Width 12.6 cm

228

Mould for coin with
inscription *Yi liu dao*

Warring States, Qi state (475–221 BC)
Length 18.8 cm, Width 10.1 cm
Handed down

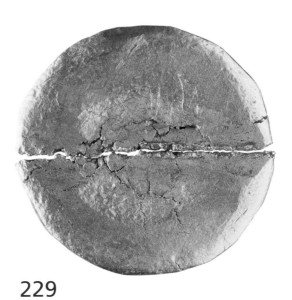

229

Gold cake

Qin (221–206 BC)
Diameter 5.8 cm, Weight 250.4 g
*Excavated in 1963 in Wujiazhun,
Lintong, Xi'an, Shaanxi Province*

230

Banliang coin

Qin (221–206 BC)
Diameter 3.6 cm, Weight 11.5 g

231

Coin with inscription *Yi wan ping wu qian*

Xinmang (9–23)

Length 7.9 cm, Width of blade 1.8 cm, Diameter of ring 2.5 cm, Weight 40 g

Handed down

232

Wuzhu **coin**

Western Han (206 BC – AD 8)

Diameter 2.5 cm, Weight 3.6 cm

Handed down

233

Spade coin with inscription *Da bu huang qian*

Xinmang (9–23)

Length 6 cm, Weight 14 g

234

Coin with inscription
Guo bao jin kui zhi wan

Xinmang (9–23)
Length 6.2 cm,
Diameter of circular part 3.1 cm
*Excavated in 1921 from site of Han
Weiyang Palace, north-west corner
city walls, Xian, Shaanxi*

This is a bronze coin with a round coin part attached to a
square base. The round part bears the inscription *Guo bao
jin kui* and the bottom section *zhi wan*, in the style of writing
under Wang Mang (r.7–23). There are different hypotheses as
to the use of this. Many palaeo-numismatists argue that it was
currency in the Wang Mang period, but many historians hold

that it was part of a tally mentioned in the histories.

There are only two and a half such items that have survived
and been handed down: one, this complete piece shown here;
one which is broken and another which has only the top part.
(Wang Liyan)

235

Gold horse hoof

Western Han (206 BC – AD 8)

Height at front 4.9 cm,
Diameter of base 6.6 cm,
Weight 250 g

Handed down

236

Gold coin with inscription '7th year of Tianxing'

Northern Wei (386–534)

Diameter 2.77 cm, Weight 16.4 g

Excavated in 1925 from the Northern Wei imperial mausoleum at Mount Mang, Luoyang, Henan Province

237

Gold *wuzhu* coin

Western Han (206 BC – AD 8)

Diameter 2.6 cm, Diameter of hole 1.1 cm

Excavated in 1980 from Xianyang, Shaanxi Province

238

Mould for *wuzhu* coins

Liang (502–557)

Dimensions 8.2 x 8.2 cm, Thickness 0.5 cm

*Excavated in December 1935 from outside
Tongji Gate, Nanjing, Jiangsu Province*

239

Coin with inscription
Kai yuan tong bao

Tang (618–907)

Diameter 2.5 cm, Weight 4.5 cm

240

Coin with inscription
Yong tong wan guo

Northern Zhou (557–581)

Diameter 3 cm, Weight c.6 g

241

Silver ingot presented as tribute by Yang Guozhong

10th year of the Tianbao reign period of Emperor
Xuanzong (751), Tang
Length 33.5 cm, Width 7.7 cm, Weight 2100 g
*Excavated in 1956 from the Tang ruin of Daming Palace in northern
Xian, Shaanxi Province*

242

Tian ce fu bao coin

Qianhua reign period, 1st year (911), Ten Kingdoms, Chu
Diameter 4.3 cm, Weight 36.6 g

This is a thick coin with a blank reverse and an inscription
around the hole on the obverse. The gold-plated coin was
minted in 911 to commemorate the promotion of Mu Yin, King
of Chu, to Supreme Commander of Tiance (*Tiance fubao*) by
Emperor Tazu of the Later Liang. The mint at Tiance produced
both copper and iron coins, which were thick and heavy with
dignified and beautiful characters. However, it had very limited
capacity and gold-plated copper coins such as this are rare,
although many lead coins have survived. (Wang Yuanxue)

244

Gold coin with inscription
Tai ping tong bao

Northern Song (960–1127)
Diameter 1.88 cm, Weight 3.5 g
Handed down

245

Coin with inscription *Da guan tong bao*

Daguan reign period (1107–1110), Northern Song
Diameter 4.1 cm, Weight 19 g

243

Coin with inscription
Da Tang zhen ku

Southern Tang (937–975)
Diameter 6 cm, Weight 93.7 g

246

Gold coin with inscription
Chun hua yuan bao

Chunhua reign period (990–994),
Northern Song

Diameter 2.4 cm, Thickness 0.12 cm,
Dimensions of hole 0.5 cm, Weight c.12 g

*Excavated in 1988 at Wutaishan,
Shanxi Province*

This is 96% pure gold. In the Chunhua period the emperor
Taizong of the Song cast coins to commemorate his visit
to Wutaishan to worship Buddha. On the obverse are the
characters 'Chunhuan Yuanbao'; on the reverse the Buddha is
shown sitting cross-legged on a lotus on the right side of the
hole and, on the left side, Sudhana stands on a lotus base with
hands together in prayer. Above is the character for the number
two. The two Buddhas are very lifelike. From the discovery
of these coins at Wutaishan, we can see the value placed on
Buddhism by the Song government. (Wang Liyan)

247

Copper two-cash coin with the inscription *Jing kang tong bao*

Jingkang reign period (1126–1127), Northern Song
Diameter 3.17 cm, Weight 7.5 g

The inscription is in regular (*kai*) script and is believed to be the calligraphy of the emperor himself. The coin has a broad margin and is finely cast. It was cast during the reign of the Northern Song emperor Qinzong but, owing to the emperor being on a campaign to the northern regions for 16 months of the Jingkang reign period, the number of coins cast during this reign period was very small, and the subset of *Jing kang tong bao* coins even fewer. Hence, because of the shortness of the reign period, the small number of coins cast and the differences between the moulds, this is an extremely rare and precious piece. This already brief reign period was subdivided into periods of different lengths, the calligraphic style of the time was changeable, and coins were produced in both copper and iron in several denominations, including one-, two- and three-cash, producing very distinctive coins. (Wang Yuanxue)

248

Coin tablet with inscription *Lin'an fu xing yong*

Southern Song (1127–1279)
Length 7.8 cm, Width 2.6 cm

250

Fifty-tael silver strip

Southern Song (1127–1279)

Height 2.9 cm, Length 14.6 cm,
Weight 1950 g

249

**Gold strip with
inscription *Wei liu lang***

Southern Song (1127–1279)

Length 12.3 cm, Width 1.4 cm,
Weight 39.4 g

*Excavated in 1956 from a theatre
construction site, Hangzhou,
Zhejiang Province*

251

Printing block for paper money

Southern Song (1127–1279)
Length 18.4 cm, Width 12.4 cm

This carved block used for printing paper money is made of copper. The five large characters running horizontally along the centre read *Xing zai kuai zi ku* (Xingzai Accounting Office Treasury). Xingzai is an alternative name for the capital Lian'an in the Southern Song (present-day Hangzhou). The text in the middle is the imperial order. The currency is decorated with a landscape scene. (Wang Liyan)

253

Coin with inscription
Tai he zhong bao

Jin (1115–1234)
Diameter 4.5 cm, Weight 20 g

252

Three-cash copper coin with inscription *Da de tong bao*

Dade reign period (1135–1139),
Western Xia (Tangut)
Diameter 2.95 cm, Weight 8.4 g

The reverse is blank while the inscription on the front is in regular (*kai*) script. The Tanguts imitated the Chinese Song system of currency production, using the traditional Chinese coin – round with a square hole, with one cash as the main denomination, but also with two-cash coins but relatively few in number. They produced both copper and iron coins and coins with Chinese and with Tangut inscriptions. The inscription on this *Da de tong bao* coin is in Chinese and it was issued, in both a large and a small type, under the Dade reign period of the Tangut emperor Chongzong. The calligraphic style is similar to the Chinese Yuande coins but with a Tangut feel.
(Wang Yuanxue)

254

Coin with inscription
Da yuan tong bao

Yuan (1271–1368)
Diameter 4 cm, Weight c. 19 g

255

Paper money: *Zhong tong yuan bao jiao chao*

Yuan (1271–1368)
Length 26.4 cm, Width 21.1 cm

256

Fifty-cash coin with Manchu and Chinese inscriptions
Xian feng zhong bao

Xianfeng reign period (1851–1861), Qing
Diameter 6 cm, Weight 80 g

257

Ten-cash coin with Manchu and Chinese inscriptions
Qi xiang zhong bao

1861, Qing
Diameter 3.5 cm, Weight c. 12.5 g

岳鄂王飛

PAINTING AND CALLIGRAPHY

The Museum's collection of calligraphy and paintings ranges in date from the Tang and Five Dynasties all the way to the modern period, but most date from the Ming and Qing late imperial period. Those items shown here generally fall into two types: the first being works by famous artists representative of their period and prominent in their times, and the second representing various historical subjects.

The Yuan was a high period for painting following the Song. The painters of this time discarded the heavy lines of earlier masters and were not fettered by realistic landscapes, but moved towards more abstraction, giving the paintings a spirit of simplicity. The painters known as 'The Four Masters of the Yuan' had an immense and lasting influence on later painters of the Ming and Qing. The paintings, *Rain in the River and Mountains*, an early work by Huang Gongwang, and *Water and Bamboo Dwelling*, one of only two extant colour paintings by Ni Zan, are of inestimable value.

The Ming was a period of great splendour in painting, seeing a growth in the institution of scholar-painters and the emergence of brilliant and varied schools of painting. *Pheasant and Camellia* by Lu Ji puts emphasis on layers of brushwork in different colours, directly carrying on a tradition from the Song period; in this way the Ming academies took on the mantle of their predecessors in the Song. By the middle of the dynasty, however, a distinct Ming style had taken over, with the Zhe or Southern School being predominant and Wen Zhengming (1470–1559) a leading representative. Together with Shen Zhou (1427–1509), Tang Yin (1470–1523) and Qiu Ying he was known as one of 'The Four Masters of the Ming' or 'The Four Masters of Wumen' (Wumen was another name for the city of Suzhou where the painters were based). The calligraphy and painting on *Dwelling to Appreciate Beauty* is delicate and refined, representing one of the new directions attempted in landscape painting in the mid Ming, during which time painting was much more an eyewitness account of life.

In the Qing the development of painting seen in the Yuan and Ming forged ahead within the limits of the influence of politics, economics, culture and thought of the time, resulting in the emergence of a particular style. Scholar-literati increasingly occupied the major role in the art world, and the various schools that emerged in the late Ming proliferated. The 'Four Wangs' – Wang Jian, Wang Shimin, Wang Hui and Wang Yuanqi – paid attention to the emotional appeal of their art and were highly esteemed by the imperial court. A new school emerged among Ming painters who had moved to the Jiangnan area in the south of China at the end of the Ming. They were critical of the Qing regime, advocated individuality, propounded new ideas and produced works full of life. Representative painters were the so-called 'Four Monks' and 'The Eight Masters of Jinling'. The Four Monks referred to Shitao, Zhuda, Hongren and Kuncan.

During the Qing, the flourishing of commerce and communications in Yangzhou resulted in a large concentration of painters, the most famous being the so-called 'Eight Eccentrics of Yangzhou': Jin Nong (1687– c.1764), Huang Shen (1687–1768), Zheng Xie (1693–1765), Li Shan (c.1686–1756), Li Fangying (1696–1755), Wang Shishen (1686–1762), Gao Xiang (1688–1753) and Luo Pin (1733–1799). Zheng Xie was known for his paintings in which bamboo, rocks and orchids merged into calligraphy.

The most representative paintings in the Museum's collections are those with historical, literary and genre subjects. *Thriving Southern Capital* and *Views of the Imperial Capital* are realistic depictions of the economic prosperity and social life in Nanjing and Beijing in the period following the Ming. *Southern Inspection Tour of Qianlong* is a major historical painting in 12 scrolls depicting the first southern inspection tour in 1751 to Zhejiang of the Qing Emperor Qianlong. The album illustrating the Qing-period novel *Strange Stories from a Chinese Studio* by Pu Songling is extremely fine and reflects the creativity fostered by the juxtaposition of literature and painting. (Zhu Min)

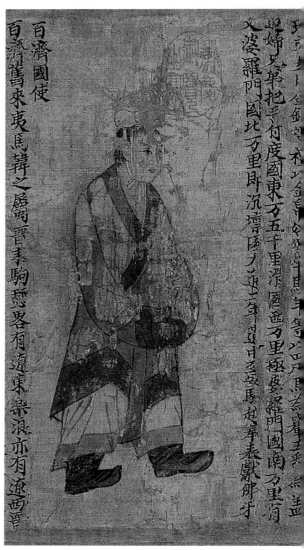

258

Eight-armed, Eleven-faced Avalokitesvara

Five Dynasties (907–960)
Banner, ink and colours on silk
Height 120 cm, Width 60.5 cm

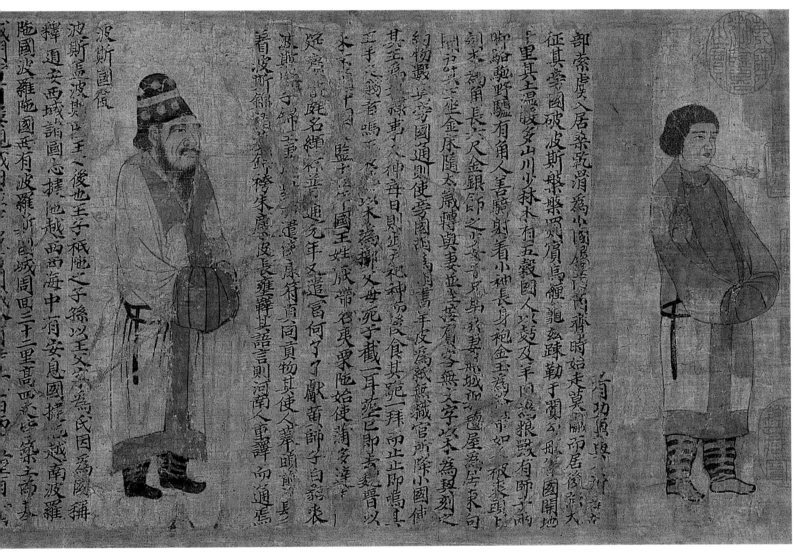

259

Offering Tribute

Northern Song (960–1127)
Scroll, ink and colours on silk
Height 25 cm, Width 198 cm

The original *Offering Tribute* was prepared on the occasion of the envoy from Jingzhou in the time of Emperor Yuan (r.552–554) of the Liang period. This one is a copy from the Northern Song period and is incomplete, the extant part showing 12 envoys, all facing to the right with details of their country's geographical location, its local customs and its relations with the Liang dynasty written behind them. The sequence is as follows (left to right): Hua Country; Persia; Paekche (one of Three Kingdoms of Korea); Qiuci (a kingdom of the Northern Taklamakan in present-day Western China); Japan; Langkasuka (in Malaysia); Dengzhi (in southern China); Zhouguke; Hebotan (Korea); Humidan; Baiti; and Moguo. The figures are depicted vividly with simple lines. The regular (*kai*) script of the explanatory text conforms to Tang-period standards. (Zhu Min)

260

The Four Generals of Zhongxing

Liu Songnian (1174–1224)
Southern Song (1127–1279)
Scroll, ink and colour on silk
Height 26 cm, Width 90.6 cm

This painting depicts four generals of the
Southern Song famous for their campaigns
against the Jurchen Jin dynasty, namely Liu
Guangshi, Han Shizhong, Zhang Jun and Yue Fei.
The full-length standing figures are formidable
and dignified, and their clothing and ornaments
are depicted with natural and fluent lines. They
are attended by their sergeants.

    There is a seven-character verse between
the figures of Zhang and Yue in the regular (*kai*)
script of the Qianlong emperor dating to 1784.
At the end of the scroll on one side is a postscript
dating to 1389 written by Yu Zhenmu. There
are also 20 imprints of imperial seals. This is an
excellent Southern Song work from the Qing
imperial collection. (Han Fulin)

261

Rain in the River and Mountains

Huang Gongwang (1269–1354)
Yuan (1271–1368)
Scroll, ink and colour on paper
Height 26.9 cm, Length 106.5 cm

262

Letter to Jingliang

Zhao Mengfu (1254–1322)

Yuan (1271–1368)

Ink on paper

Height of folio 29 cm, Width of folio 11.5 cm

264

Dwelling to Appreciate Beauty

Wen Zhengming (1470–1559)

Ming (1368–1644)

Scroll, ink and colours on paper

Height of painting 28.6 cm, Length 79 cm

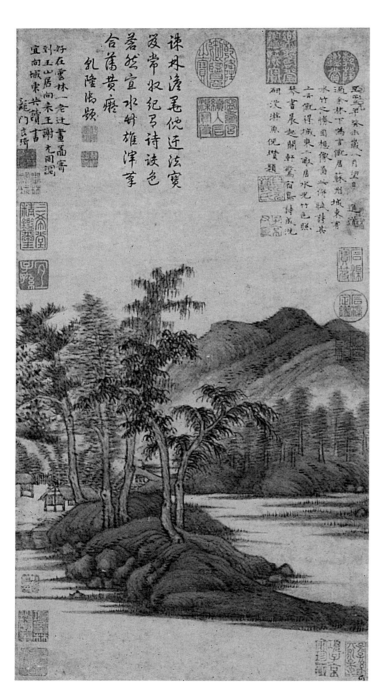

263

Water and Bamboo Dwelling

Ni Zan (1301–1374)

Yuan (1271–1368)

Hanging scroll, ink and colour on paper

Height 53.6 cm, Width 27.7 cm

265

Views of the Imperial Capital

Anonymous, 1609
Ming (1368–1644)
Scroll, ink and colours on silk
Height 32 cm, Length 2182.6 cm

The scene shows the imperial capital of Beijing during the
Ming on a grand occasion. Farmers, artisans, peddlers with
their stalls, entertainers, diviners and astrologers, officials and
military are shown among a setting of farmland and wilderness,
with villages and towns, streets and markets, temples, bridges,
palaces, official buildings, rivers, mountains and passes and
rivers, the whole ingeniously contrived to create vivid and
natural scenes of urban social life. There is a colophon by Weng
Zhengchun at the end of the scroll dating to 1609. (Han Fulin)

266

Pheasant and Camellia

Lu Ji (1477–?)
Ming (1368–1644)
Hanging scroll, ink and colour on silk
Height 185 cm, Width 109 cm

267

Thriving Southern Capital

Anonymous
Ming (1368–1644)
Scroll, ink and colours on silk
Height 44 cm, Length 350 cm

The whole scroll depicts scenes from Nanjing life at the latter
part of the Ming period. It shows the prosperity, the diversity
of urban life and the richness of cultural life. It is an important
historical document for researching the economic development
of handicrafts and commerce in Nanjing, providing data on
communications, accommodation, clothing, food and drink.
(Zhu Min)

268

River and Mountains

Wang Jian (1598–1677)
Qing (1644–1911)
Hanging scroll, ink and pigments on paper
Height 220.7, Width 104.8 cm

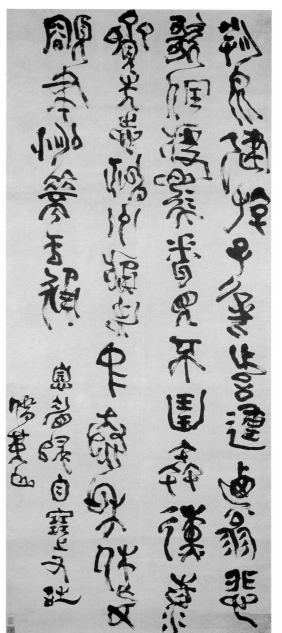

269

Poem on a Mountain Pass

Fu Shan (1605–1690)

Qing (1644–1911)

Hanging scroll, ink on paper

Height 208.5 cm, Width 84.3 cm

270

White Clouds and Brocade Trees

Gong Xian (c.1618–1689)
Qing (1644–1911)
Hanging scroll, ink and pigments on silk
Height 183.5 cm, Width 47 cm

271

Deer and Pine

Zhu Da (c.1626–1705)
Qing (1644–1911)
Hanging scroll, ink and wash on paper
Height 182 cm, Width 91.4 cm

272

Daoist in the Mountains among the Plum Blossoms

Shitao (1642–1707)
Qing (1644–1911)
Hanging scroll, ink and wash on silk
Height 87.5 cm, Width 51.2 cm

273

Mountain Dwelling West of the River

Hua Yan (1682–c.1762)
Qing (1644–1911)
Hanging scroll, ink and colour on paper
Height 171.5 cm, Width 85.8 cm

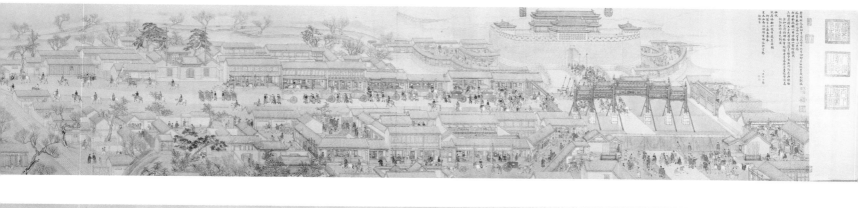

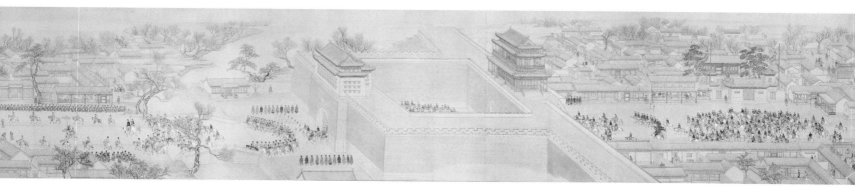

274

Southern Inspection Tour of Qianlong

Xu Yang (act. 1750–76), 1776
Qing (1644–1911)
Scroll, ink and colour on paper
First scroll: Height 68.6 cm, Width 1988.6 cm

Southern Inspection Tour of Qianlong is a set of scrolls commissioned as a historical record of the first southern inspection tour in 1751 to Zhejiang of the Qing Emperor Gaozong, Qianlong, made in the 16th year of the Qianlong reign period. The tour lasted 112 days and covered over 5800 *li*. The painting was prepared on imperial order under the direction of the palace artist Xu Yang and comprised 12 scrolls: Beijing: Zhengyang Gate to Liangxiang County; Dezhou, Shandong; Crossing the Yellow River; Confluence of Huai and Yellow Rivers; Crossing the Yangzi from Jinshan to Jiaoshan; Entering Suzhou from North of Tiger Mountain; Jiangsu–Zhenjiang Border; Huangzhou and the West Lake; Shaoxing and the Yu Temple; Military Inspection at Nanjing; Confluence of Yellow and Huai Rivers; Beijing: Zhonghua Gate to Duan

Gate. The scrolls were completed on silk in 1770 and in 1776 Xu Yang completed a duplicate version on paper. Scrolls 1, 7, 8 and 11 of the original silk scrolls are now lost and this is the paper duplicate of scroll 1.

The scrolls show the use of traditional painting techniques to capture the character and style of the southern countryside and towns, including the Yellow, Huai, He and Yangtze rivers, West Lake and South Lake, and other famous scenic spots. At the same time, it depicted the south in the early Qianlong period, including local customs, the role of magistrates, inspection of rivers, inspection of troops, sacrificing to the ancestors at mountains, and sightseeing. It shows the reality of 18th-century politics, economics, culture and society. (Zhu Min)

275

Three Wishes of Hua Feng

Zheng Xie (1693–1765)
Qing (1644–1911)
Hanging scroll, ink and wash on paper
Height 167.7, Width 92.7 cm

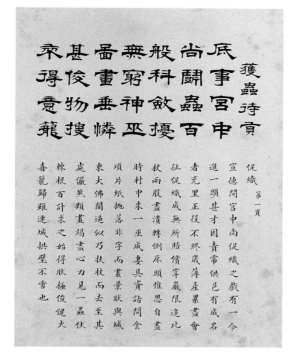

276

Illustrated *Strange Stories from a Chinese Studio*

Anonymous
Qing (1644–1911)
Album leaves, ink and colours on paper
Height 52 cm, Width 38 cm

This is an illustrated version of the Qing-period novel *Strange Stories from a Chinese Studio* by Pu Songling. Consisting in total of 48 albums, 46 are extant. The albums have a folding or concertina form with wooden covers, with brocade mounted on the base, and four large characters on the top right reading 'Album of Chinese Studio' and, at the bottom, the title of the chapters in small characters. There are 420 stories in the book, with 725 illustrations, some stories with only one illustration and some with as many as five, with text and illustration on facing pages. The text side has a poem at the top

and the extract from the story below, creating a harmonious combination and images and resulting in a work of art.

The album was created at the end of the Qing period and presented to the court. Although organized by Xu Run, it was work of several famous masters. In 1900 when forces of the Eight Allied Powers invaded China the album was carried off by the Tsarist forces of imperial Russia. It remained in Russia until 19 April 1958, when it was returned to China by the Committee for Cultural Relations with Foreign Countries of the former Soviet Union. (Zhu Min)

PICTORIAL BRICKS

Pictorial bricks were made by stamping or moulding the patterns or a scene on building brick. They have a history of over ten centuries from the end of the Warring States period to the Yuan period. Over this time society had undergone enormous changes, especially following changes of political regime, and the thousands of pictorial bricks discovered to date not only provide a vivid record of the reality of life and its changes, but also reveal the development of this popular art.

The National Museum holds items dating from the Eastern Han through to the Song dynasty. They are rich in content and format and have historical, literary and artistic worth.

The Eastern Han bricks excavated in Pengxian in Sichuan Province skilfully express a feeling of realism, vividly depicting all aspects of Han-period society – politics, economics, culture, art and ideology. They show scenes from agriculture, business, handicrafts and trade, such as sowing, harvesting, picking mulberries, gathering lotuses, salt collection, boiling salt, hunting, market trading, pounding rice and fermenting vinegar. They give a visual historical record and are an important source for research on the society of the time.

A large-format stone picture showing *Banquets and Music, Chariots and Horses* was excavated in 1954 from tomb No. 1, Yangzishan, Chengdu in Sichuan Province, composed of eight large slabs with a total length of 11.3 m, like a long scroll. The bricks excavated from the Southern dynasties tombs at Dengxian, Henan Province, are of even size and have been stamped and then painted. The compositions are compact with long and slender – yet animated – figures and with bold decorative lines. The bricks are painted in seven colours, including red, green and purple. There are three genres of scene: those showing chariots and riders, including warhorses, warriors and imperial carriages; those depicting auspicious creatures such as the phoenix, *qilin* (a mythical Chinese animal) and heavenly horses; and those showing Buddhist flying deities – apsarsas. These are important for the study of Eastern Jin and Southern dynasties art, clothing and personal adornment. (Yu Lu)

277
Brick depicting the pounding of rice

Eastern Han (25–220)

Height 25 cm, Length 39 cm

*Excavated in 1959 from Pengxian,
Sichuan Province*

278

Brick depicting hunting and fishing

Eastern Han (25–220)

Length 45 cm, Width 41 cm, Thickness 6.8 cm

Excavated in 1954 from Yangzishan, Chengdu, Sichuan Province

279

Brick depicting wine brewing

Eastern Han (25–220)

Length 38.5 cm, Width 28 cm, Thickness 5.7 cm

Excavated in 1954 from Pengxian, Sichuan Province

280

Brick depicting salt panning

Eastern Han (25–220)

Length 41.2 cm, Width 46.5 cm, Thickness 6 cm

Excavated in 1954 from Yangzishan, Chengdu, Sichuan Province

282

Brick depicting an orchard
of wood-oil trees

Eastern Han (25–220)
Height 24 cm, Width 37.4 cm
*Excavated in 1954 from Pengxian,
Sichuan Province*

281

Brick depicting a market
with storied buildings

Eastern Han (25–220)
Height 28 cm, Width 48 cm
*Excavated from Guanghan,
Sichuan Province*

283

Brick depicting a kitchen scene

Eastern Han (25–220)

Height 25 cm, Width 40 cm

Acquired in 1956 from Deyang, Sichuan Province

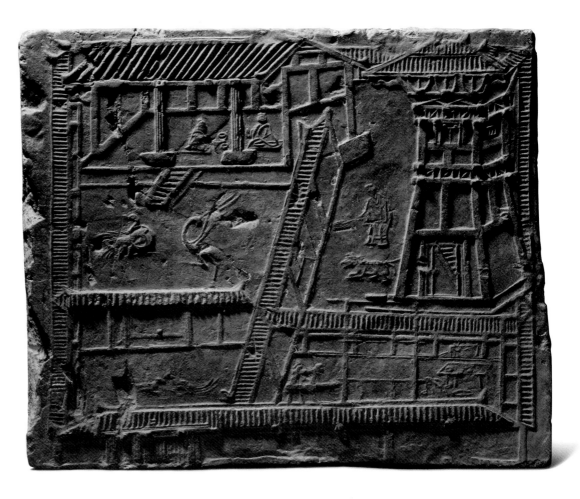

284

Brick depicting a courtyard house

Eastern Han (25–220)

Height 40 cm, Width 46.4 cm, Thickness 6.3 cm

Excavated in 1954 from Yangzishan, Chengdu, Sichuan Province

285

Brick depicting a war supply chariot

Eastern Han (25–220)

Height 39 cm, Width 46.5 cm, Thickness 5.4 cm

Excavated in 1953 from Yangzishan, Chengdu, Sichuan Province

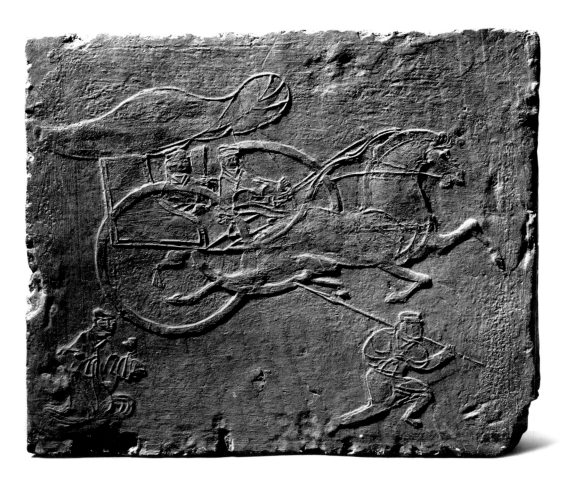

286

Brick depicting entertainers

Eastern Han (25–220)

Length 40 cm, Width 40 cm

Excavated in 1954 from Yangzishan, Chengdu, Sichuan Province

287

Brick depicting chariots with tightrope walkers and riders

Eastern Han (25–220)

Length 105.5 cm, Width 35.6 cm, Thickness 6.7 cm

Excavated in 1988 from Fanji, Xinyexian, Henan Province

The picture is in two sections. The right part shows a procession of chariots and riders while the left depicts a chariot tightrope show. Tightrope walking was a popular entertainment in the Han period, but that done balanced on chariots was the most difficult. There are two chariots shown here, each with one upright pole, a man sitting on top of the front one holding the rope in one hand. A man is climbing the pole in the rear chariot and there is another man hanging upside down from the rope. The chariots, uprights and rope are all interlinked, meaning that the swaying of the two chariots and of the rope causes considerable movement, making for thrilling entertainment. (Yu Lu)

288

Brick depicting a phoenix

Southern dynasties (420–589)

Length 38.7 cm, Width 18.9 cm, Thickness 6.3 cm

Excavated in 1958 from Dengxian, Henan Province

289

Brick depicting aristocratic women on an outing

Southern dynasties (420–589)

Length 38 cm, Width 19 cm, Thickness 6.3 cm

Excavated in 1958 from Dengxian, Henan Province

290

Brick depicting a woman
putting up her hair

Song (960–1279)

Height 37.3 cm, Width 11.3 cm,
Thickness 2.1 cm

*Excavated from Yanshi,
Henan Province*

291

Brick depicting a woman washing

Song (960–1279)

Height 39 cm, Width 16 cm, Thickness 1.9 cm

Excavated from Yanshi, Henan Province

292

Brick depicting a woman gutting fish

Song (960–1279)

Height 34.2 cm, Width 24.1 cm, Thickness 2.2 cm

Excavated from Yanshi, Henan Province

293

Brick depicting a Chinese opera competition

Song (960–1279)

Height 28.4 cm, Width 9.3 cm

OTHER COLLECTIONS

Oracle bones are inscribed turtle plastrons and animal bones dating from the Shang period. The inscriptions recorded the divination of the Shang kings and reveal aspects of politics, economics, military affairs, culture and society and make them a very valuable historical source. They were found in the site of the last capital of the Shang dynasty, Yinxu, near Anyang in Henan Province. The Museum has over 400 pieces, some of which have been published by Luo Zhenyu and Wang Guowei in their major reference works on oracle bones, and others coming from the collections of He Sui, Yao Jian, Yu Xingwu, Tang Lan and Yao Huazhu. The bone recording the invasions of the Tufang peoples and the *Way of the King* turtle plastron both record events at the time of the Shang emperor, Wu Ding (r.1198–1189 BC), and are important historical documents. The characters of the inscriptions on the former are smeared with cinnabar to make them stand out. The latter records the divination of the disaster of Wu Ding taking on a military role. The bone ladle made from a slaughtered animal uses inlaid turquoise for the decorative motifs while the densely positioned characters in the orderly inscription shows the mature style of Shang oracle bone calligraphy.

Chime stones are musical instruments from classical times and the museum has both unusual stones and a complete set of stones, originally hung from a beam, dating from the whole of pre-modern Chinese history. The tiger chime stone excavated from the Shang Yinxu ruins at Anyang is enormous and very heavy, considered to be the king of Shang chime stones. Scientific analysis has shown that this sounds five musical scales and so can be used to play different compositions.

Although relatively small, the Museum's collection of stone sculptures contains many fine pieces. Yang Sixu was the trusted eunuch general of the Tang emperor Xuanzong (r.713–55), repeatedly excelling in military life, and the gilded stone figure from his tomb depicting a warrior could be seen as a portrayal of the imperial bodyguard in his lifetime. The delicately modelled painted relief sculpture of a Heavenly King with gold is one of two originally flanking the tomb door of Wang Chuzhi, a military governor in the Tang. It was previously owned by the American collector, R. H. Ellsworth, but after learning of the thefts from this tomb he gave the statue to the museum.

The Wanli reign period (1573–1620) black lacquered medicine chest with dragons outlined in gold was used in the imperial pharmacy. It has an ingenious design, using a combination of rotating and fixed drawers, enabling storage of as many as 140 medicines and making it easy to use.

The museum's seal collection is varied and rich, although the greatest number are bronze. Before the Qin period both official and private seals were known by a single term, *xi*. The jade seal of the feudal lord of the Chu state is a famous seal of the Warring States period. After the Qin state united China under the First Emperor, they introduced regulations governing the making of seals and only emperors were allowed a 'ruler's seal' or *xi*, whereas ministers, nobles and those lower in rank were allowed to use seals called *yin* and *zhang*. The Qin-period *yin* seal of Gongsun Gu is valuable evidence of this system. Among the Museum's collection of Han-period *yin* seals, the gold seal of the King of Dian is a legacy of the political power of the ancient state in south-west China. Research on the jade seal of the Prince of Huaiyang has revealed it to have been used by the son of the Western Han emperor Xuandi (r.73–49 BC) and his own children. The signature seal became prevalent in the Yuan period as officials who were Mongolians or who belonged to diverse ethnicities grouped in this period into the Semu peoples (which included Turks, Persians, Arabs and many others) could not write their own signature and so used a seal like this; these were conferred by the emperor and not allowed to be used by others. The Ming wooden seal of the imperial guard has lost its handle/knob but the carving is still distinct and it is in relatively good condition, surprising given its age. The Qing jade imperial seal is an emblem of imperial power, one of 25 imperial seals of the Qianlong emperor (r.1736–95) and distinctive of its time with matching Manchu and Chinese inscriptions. (Sheng Weiren)

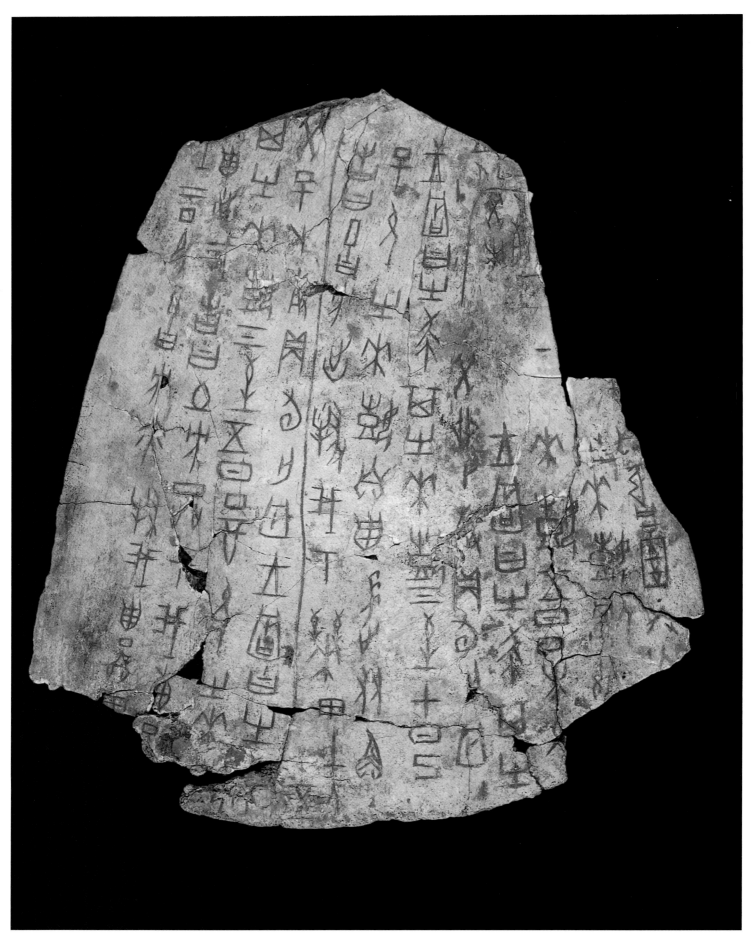

FRONT

BACK

294

Oracle bone recording the
invasion of the Tufang peoples

Shang (1600–1046 BC)
Length 22.5 cm, Width 19 cm
*Excavated from Yinxu, Anyang,
Henan Province*

The long inscription on both sides of this oracle bone consists
of 170 characters, inscribed vertically and highlighted with
cinnabar: the colour remains vivid. The inscription records
various matters including a kingly edict for a hunt by the feudal
lords, celestial phenomenon and an invasion. It is an important
source for the study of Shang society and the history of
astronomy. (Han Fulin)

295

Turtle plastron with inscription with 'The way of the king'

Shang (1600–1046 BC)

Length 18.6 cm, Width 10.2 cm

Excavated from Yinxu, Anyang, Henan Province

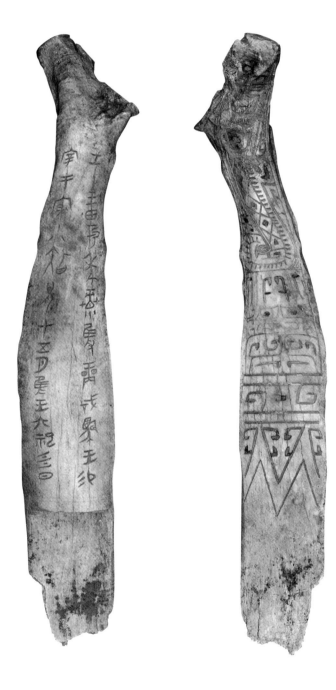

296

Bone ladle made from a slaughtered animal

Shang (1600–1046 BC)

Length 27.3 cm, Width 3.8 cm

Excavated from Yinxu, Anyang, Henan Province

297

Tiger pattern chime stone

Shang (1600–1046 BC)
Length 84 cm, Width 42 cm, Thickness 2.5 cm
Excavated in 1950 from Yinxu, Anyang, Henan Province

Stone chimes have been found in Neolithic sites in China,
and many were also found in the last Shang capital at Yinxu,
including five long ones from the tomb of Fu Hao (consort of
emperor Wu Ding) that have particularly fine workmanship and
are inscribed with characters and owl patterns. Among these
are three made of white jade muddy limestone, of a similar
shape and possibly forming a set. The large tiger pattern chime
stone shown here could be called the king of Shang chime
stones. It is inscribed with a robust tiger and has been shown
to sound five musical scales, thus could be used for performing
different compositions. It is invaluable for understanding
Chinese musical history. (Yu Lu)

298

Gilded stone statue of soldier

Tang (618–907)
Height 40.5 cm
Excavated in 1958 from Yang Sixu's tomb, Xian, Shaanxi Province

Yang Sixu, who died in 740, was the eunuch general to the Tang emperor Xuanzong (r.713–55). This figure from his tomb is wearing typical Tang clothing. He carries two sets of battle equipment, comprising sheathed swords, and bows and arrows in a sheath. One set is more refined and decorated with gold, clearly intended for his master, while the other set is for his own use. The warrior has a martial yet respectful bearing and is intended as an honour guard for Yang Sixu for his afterlife. The statue is made from white marble but much of the original gilding has flaked away. In its form and spirit and fine finish it is representative of Tang stone sculpture. (Yu Lu)

299

Heavenly King

Five Dynasties (907–960)

Height 113.5 cm, Width 58 cm,
Thickness 11.7 cm

Gifted in 2000 by R. H. Ellsworth

The Heavenly King is a Buddhist symbol, protector of the faith. This bold and powerful piece painted with red and ochre was sculpted from a rectangular slab of white marble. This tomb guardian wears a gilded helmet and armour. His eyes wide open, he stands on a prone deer holding a double-edged sword, which pierces a lotus flower that is impaled on the deer's antlers. A blue dragon on his head and shoulders holds a precious pearl, a Buddhist symbol, in its mouth. The statue is influenced by the techniques of the preceding Tang period, including the use of relief, but has a heightened sense of realism and atmosphere. Five Dynasties grave sites in northern China are extremely rare and this piece is of high artistic value, and is a treasure for the study of ancient painting and carving. (Su Qiang)

300

Wanli-period gold-inlaid black lacquer imperial medicine chest

Wanli reign period (1573–1620), Ming
Height 94.1 cm, Length 78.9 cm, Width 57 cm

301

**Jade seal of the feudal
lord of the Chu state**

Warring States (475–221 BC)

Height 2.1 cm, Width 2.5 cm,
Weight 20 g

302

Jade seal: 'Gongsun Gu's seal'

Qin (221–206 BC)

Height 1.6 cm, Width 2.2 cm, Weight 18 g

303

Gold seal: 'Seal of the King of Dian'

Western Han (206 BC – AD 8)
Height 1.8 cm, Width 2.4 cm, Weight 89.5 g.
Excavated in 1956 from the King of Dian's tomb, Zhaishan, Pudingxian, Yunnan Province

Made of gold with a snake handle, this square seal is inscribed with four characters 'Seal of the King of Dian'. The workmanship is refined and the inscription uses the distinctive square and smooth strokes of seal script in its Qin-dynasty form. (Zhang Runping)

304

Gold seal

Western Han (206 BC – AD 8)
Height 1.8 cm, Length 2.4 cm
Handed down after being found at Richao, Shandong Province

305

Silver seal of a general

Northern and Southern dynasties (420–589)

Height 2 cm, Width 2.3 cm, Weight 67 g

306

Jade seal: 'Seal of the Prince of Huaiyang'

Western Han (206 BC – AD 8)

Height 1.6 cm, Width 2.2 cm, Weight 20 g

307

Bronze seal: 'Yu Hou's Vermillion seal'

Ruigong reign period, 2nd year (989), Song

Height 5.8 cm, Width 5.4 cm, Weight 640 g

308

Bronze seal: 'Official seal of the
Cavalry Officer of the Southern
Division of Hedong'

Jin 1172

Length 7 cm, Width 7 cm

309

Dragon-handle jade
signature seal

Yuan (1271–1368)

Height 4.8 cm, Width 4.2 cm

310

Jade imperial seal

Qianlong emperor (1736–1795), Qing

Height 15.7 cm, Length 16.2 cm,
Width 15.8 cm

311

Wood seal of the Ming Imperial
Guard (the Brocade Guards)

Chenghua reign period, 14th year (1478), Ming

Height 4.2 cm, Length 11.5 cm, Width 10.9 cm,
Weight 200 g

中華民國

和國臨時中央政府佈告

第一號

MODERN CHINA

The National Museum of China is formed from combining the original Museum of the Chinese Revolution and the Museum of Chinese History. The present museum has over 200,000 objects dating from the Opium Wars of 1840 onwards to the present day, which formed the basis of the Museum of the Chinese Revolution. Among them are 2,220 First Rank Cultural Objects, forming the greatest modern and contemporary collections of present-day museums in China. These collections reflect the major events and important figures of modern Chinese history, and most especially the Chinese Communist Party's role in leading the democratic and social revolutions of the Chinese people, in the construction of a history of and testimony to the most recent century of progress of the Chinese people. (Chen Yu)

旨朕欽奉

隆裕皇太后懿旨前因民軍起事各省響應九夏沸騰

生靈塗炭特命袁世凱遣員與民軍代表討論大局

議開國會公決政體兩月以來尚無確當辦法南北

暌隔彼此相持商輟於途士露於野徒以國體一日

不決故民生一日不安今全國人民心理多傾向共

和南中各省既倡議於前北方諸將亦主張於後人

心所嚮天命可知予亦何忍因一姓之尊榮拂兆民

之好惡是用外觀大勢內審輿情特率皇帝將統治

權公諸全國定為共和立憲國體近慰海內厭亂望

治之心遠協古聖天下為公之義袁世凱前經資政

院選舉為總理大臣當茲新舊代謝之際宜有南北

統一之方即由袁世凱以全權組織臨時共和政府

與民軍協商統一辦法總期人民安堵海宇乂安仍

合滿漢蒙回藏五族完全領土為一大中華民國予

與皇帝得以退處寬閒優游歲月長受國民之優禮

親見郅治之告成豈不懿歟欽此

宣統三年[印]十二月二十五日

內閣總理大臣臣 袁世凱

署外務大臣臣 胡惟德

民政大臣臣 趙秉鈞

署度支大臣臣 紹英

學務大臣臣 唐景崇

陸軍大臣臣 王士珍

署海軍大臣臣 譚學衡

司法大臣臣 沈家本

著農工商大臣臣 熙彥

署郵傳大臣臣 梁士詒

理藩大臣臣 達壽

312

Edict Announcing Emperor Puyi's Abdication

12 February 1912
Height 21.5 cm, Length 53 cm
Ink on paper
Handed over by Beijing Normal University

In October 1911 there was an uprising in Wuchang on the Yangtze River, which was suppressed by the Qing dynasty under the leadership of General Yuan Shikai. As a result, Yuan Shikai arranged the abdication of the last Qing emperor, Puyi, and negotiated with the revolutionaries to become President of the new Republic of China. The abdication edict was issued on 12 February 1912, bringing two thousand years of imperial China to an end. The edict, drafted by Zhang Jian, was first debated in the Nanjing Provisional Senate before being passed on by Yuan Shikai and announced by the Qing. (Wan Ting)

313

The Communist: Monthly magazine
published by the Shanghai Communist Party

1920

Height 25.5cm, Width 18.5 cm

Printing on paper

Transferred to the History Reference Room,
Propaganda Department of the Chinese Communist
Party Central Committee, in April 1953

The Communist was first published by the Shanghai Communist
Party on 7 November 1920, as a semi-public monthly magazine,
with Li Daren as its editor. For the first time the Communist
Party flag was raised in China. The magazine introduced Marxist
theory and clarified the ideas of the Chinese Communist
Party. It had a circulation of up to 5,000 and was intended to
promote the expansion of the Party. In July 1921, after only
six issues, it was forced to suspend publication. Issue 1, shown
here, describes Lenin, the Communist parties in Russia, Britain
and elsewhere, and the Third International. (Liu Yanbo)

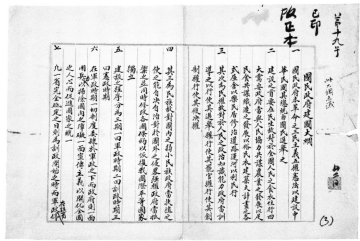

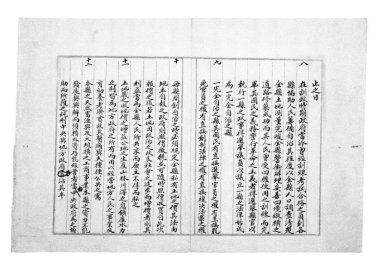

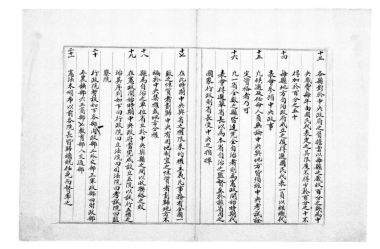

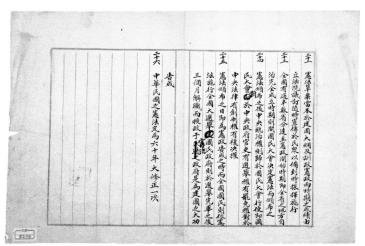

314

Manuscript copy of *Fundamentals of National Reconstruction*

1924

Height 21.2 cm, Width 30 cm

Brush on paper. Four leaves, annotation in Sun Yatsen's hand, 'Corrections for printer'

Transferred to the Shanghai Committee of the Chinese Communist Party Central Committee on 1 August 1964

The first National Congress of the Chinese Nationalist Party, or Guomindang, held on 20 January 1924 approved a new constitution, drafted by Sun Yatsen in 25 articles. This included the Three Principles of the People – establishment of a government of the people, by the people, and for the people – the government to comprise five branches, the Executive, Legislative, Judicial, Examination and Control. The process of revolutionary construction was divided into three periods: military, training and constitutional governance. In the proposal Sun Yatsen noted that one aim of the Congress was to reorganize the military government into a National People's Government. Although the main points adopted by the Congress were the same as in this manuscript, the final text was slightly different. (Liu Yanbo)

315

Announcement of the Interim Government of the China Soviet Republic (No. 1)

December 1931
Height 52.6 cm, Width 73.8 cm
Lithographic printing on paper, fragments
Handed over by Fujian Province Cultural Artefacts Committee in 1951

From 7 to 20 November 1931, the China Soviet Republic convened for the first national meeting of its representatives in Yeping, Ruijin in Jiangxi Province. There were 610 representatives from Soviet and White areas present. They announced that the China Soviet Republic was established as the Provisional Central Government with its capital in Ruijin. It issued its first edict on 1 December, announcing that Mao Zedong and 63 others would form the Central Executive Committee as well as details of the first meeting of the Executive, explaining the nature of the Provisional Central Government and the Central Executive Committee. (Yao Jie)

316

Camera used by Edgar Snow in Bao'an

1936
Height 12.4 cm, Length 22 cm, Width 5.5 cm
Metal case, glass lens
Presented by Mrs D. E. Alexander on 27 April 1979

Edgar Parks Snow (1905–1972) was a famous American writer and journalist. In 1928 he was sent to China as a journalist. In June 1936 he left Beiping (now Beijing) for Xian and moved on to Bao'an, Shannxi Province, capital of the Communist-held areas of China at that time and site of the Communist Party's Central Committee's headquarters. Over a four-month period he met many of the Communist leaders. His later book, *Red Flag Over China*, reported for the first time from a Western perspective the situation in the revolutionary area. Before leaving Beiping, Snow had borrowed a 16-mm camera from a fellow-journalist and teacher at Yenching (Yanjing) University, James White, and used it to depict the activities of Mao Zedong, Zhou Enlai and other leaders of the Red Army, creating an immensely important historical record. In October 1936 Snow was back in Beiping and returned the camera to White. White returned temporarily to the States in 1940 and gave this camera to his sister, D. E. Alexander, who presented it to the Museum in 1979. (Yao Jie)

317

Octagonal cap worn by Mao Zedong when in the Red Army in Bao'an

1936
Diameter at opening 57 cm
Grey cloth
Presented in October 1975 to the
State Administration of Cultural Relics

When the American journalist Edgar Snow was taking photographs of Mao Zedong between July and October 1936 in the Revolutionary Area at Bao'an (present-day Zhidan County), he offered his own Red Army eight-cornered cap to Mao Zedong as Mao was not wearing one. Snow later took this cap back to the States. In September 1975, Snow's widow, Lois Wheeler Snow, was invited to visit China, and presented this cap as a gift from the whole family to China. (Yao Jie)

318

**Legal robe worn by Mei Ru-ao
in the Tokyo War Crimes Tribunal**

May 1946 to April 1948
Length 124.3 cm
Silk
Gifted by Mei Ru-ao's family in 1998

Mei Ru-ao (1904–1973) was from Nanchang in Jiangxi Province.
He received his doctorate in law from Chicago University
and afterwards worked as a law professor at Shanxi and
other universities. In 1934 he was a member of the Chinese
Legislative Yuan, acting as Chair for the Foreign Affairs
Committee. In February 1946, he was appointed by General
MacArthur, along with ten other legal representatives from
countries including the USA, Russia and the UK, to sit on a
panel of judges for the International Military Tribunal for the
Far East, also known as the Tokyo War Crimes Tribunal. He
acted according to the law, arguing for justice for the Chinese
people in order to safeguard their sovereignty and dignity.

This is the legal robe worn by Mei Ru-ao for the Tribunal.
In June 1949 he sent the gown to Hong Kong but it was
returned to China at the end of the year. (An Li)

319

*Judgment: International Military
Tribunal of the Far East* (English text)

1946–1948
Height 33 cm, Width 20.3 cm
9 fascicules, ink on paper, English
Gifted by Mei Ru-ao's family in 1998

On 19 January 1946, the International Military Tribunal of the
Far East was established by General MacArthur, the Supreme
Commander of the Allied Powers, to try the leaders of the
Empire of Japan for war crimes. The judges were chosen by
MacArthur from among candidates nominated by the Allied
Powers. The trials were held in Tokyo, with the prosecution
starting on 3 May 1946, and continued until 12 November
1948. The 1,781-page judgment was drafted by the judges
from seven countries and included sections totalling 300 pages
relevant to China drafted by Mei Ru-ao and his aides providing
strong evidence. Mei Ru-ao took this part of the judgment to
Hong Kong in June 1949 and handed it over to the collection
of the calligrapher Liu Yong'An. (An Li)

320

**The flag raised by Mao Zedong
at the Proclamation of the
People's Republic of China**

1 October 1949

Height 338 cm, Width 460 cm

Red silk, yellow satin, rolled steel (on large star)

*Handed over by the People's Government of
Beijing Municipality on 1 July 1957*

At 3 pm on 1 October 1949, in front of a crowd of 300,000
soldiers and civilians in Tiananmen Square, there was a ceremony
to celebrate the establishment of the People's Republic of China
(PRC). Chairman Mao Zedong pressed a button, which caused the
flag to rise on a flagpole in the north of the square, a symbol of the
establishment of the PRC. (Ji Ruxun)

321

The Founding Ceremony

1953

Dong Xiwen (1914–1973), Professor at
the China Central Fine Arts College

230 x 450 cm

Oil painting

322

Seal of the People's Government of the People's Republic of China

1949

Seal 9 x 9 cm, Thickness 2.7 cm,
Length of handle 10.9 cm

Bronze

*Transferred in May 1959 by the
Secretariat of the State Council*

On 30 September 1949, at the first plenary session of the
China Communist Party Central Committee, Mao Zedong
was elected Chairman of the People's Republic of China.
He officially took office on 1 October 1949. The seal shown
here was approved by the Central People's Government and
was used to provide proof of ratification of laws, decrees,
policies, treaties and orders.

The square seal is cut with characters in Song script
reading 'Seal of the Central People's Government of The
People's Republic of China'. It is engraved with the lines,
'Seal No. 1, 1 November 1949, The Central People's
Government of the People's Republic of China'. (Ji Ruxun)

323

**Crystal Bald Eagle given to
Deng Xiaoping by Ronald Reagan**

April 1984

Height 12 cm, Length 18.5 cm,
Width 8.5 cm

Crystal glass

Presented on 16 October 1985

The American president, Ronald W. Reagan, made an official state visit to China between 26 April and 1 May 1984, the first since the establishment of diplomatic relations between America and China in 1979. On 28 April the Chairman of the Central Advisory Committee and Head of the Central Military Committee of the Chinese Communist Party, Deng Xiaoping, received him in the Great Hall of the People. Reagan presented Deng Xiaoping with gifts, including this crystal Bald Eagle, the national emblem of the United States. (Ji Ruxun)

324

Olympic Gold Medal
of Xu Haifeng

29 July 1984
Diameter 6 cm
Gold-plated silver
Donated by Xu Haifeng on 14 October 1984

The 23rd Olympic Games were held in Los Angeles between
28 July and 12 August 1984 and China, for the first time since
1952, sent a team to compete. On the first day of competition
on 29 July, Xu Haifeng (1957–), won the men's 50-m pistol
competition. This is the first gold medal of those games, but
also represents China's Olympic medal 'breakthrough'. In these
Olympic Games, China won a total of 15 golds, eight silver
and nine bronze medals, coming fourth in the medal table.
(Ji Ruxun)

326

Wooden gavel used to announce China's membership of the World Trade Organization

13 November 2001
Length 32.2 cm
Wood
Gifted by Beijing Daily Newspaper Group on 12 December 2001

The World Trade Organization (WTO) was established on 1 January 1995, formerly known as the General Agreement on Tariffs and Trade. From 1986 China made great efforts in bilateral and multilateral negotiations to become a contracting member. On 13 November 2001, at the fourth WTO Ministerial Conference in Doha, the President of the General Assembly and Minister of Finance, Economy and Commerce of Qatar, Mr Yousef Hussain Kamal, banged the gavel to announce that China had become a WTO member. After the meeting, the *Beijing Evening News* announced that its meeting's staff had acquired the gavel for its special significance. (An Li)

325

Fountain pen used by Liu Qi, Head of the Chinese Delegation to host the 2008 Olympic Games

13 July 2001
Length 13.5 cm
Metal and plastic
Presented on 4 June 2002

In 1991, Beijing applied again to the International Olympic Committee to host the 29th Olympic Games in 2008. It received the support of the public and all levels of government and, at the vote by the 112th Plenary Meeting of the Committee on 13 July 2001, Beijing won a majority in the second round to host the Games. Liu Qi, Head of the Beijing delegation, signed the agreement with this pen. It has the five-ring Olympic symbol on its cap. (An Li)